FORT LANCASTER

FORT LANCASTER

Texas Frontier Sentinel

By Lawrence John Francell

TEXAS STATE
HISTORICAL ASSOCIATION

Library of Congress Cataloging-in-Publication Data

Francell, Lawrence John.
    Fort Lancaster : Texas frontier sentinel / by Lawrence John Francell.
        p.   cm.   — (Fred Rider Cotten popular history series; no. 13)
    Includes bibliographical references.
    ISBN 0-87611-173-8 (pbk.)
        1. Fort Lancaster (Tex.)—History.   2. Frontier and pioneer life—Texas.
        3. Texas—History, Military—19th century.   I. Title.   II. Series.
    F394.F637F73   1999
    976.4'875—dc21   98-54581
                                                                                CIP

© 1999 by the Texas Parks and Wildlife Department.
All rights reserved. Printed in the U.S.A.
Number thirteen in the Fred Rider Cotten Popular History Series.

Published by the Texas State Historical Association in cooperation with the Center
for Studies in Texas History at the University of Texas at Austin.

Cover: Ruins, enlisted men's barracks, Fort Lancaster State Historic Site, 1972.
Photograph courtesy Texas Department of Transportation, Austin, Texas.

CONTENTS

INTRODUCTION

ON AUGUST 20, 1855, one hundred and six men of Companies H and K of the First Infantry Regiment arrived at a preselected site on Live Oak Creek in West Texas. Their task was to establish Camp Lancaster, the newest link in a chain of forts providing protection for the southern overland route to California. Fort Lancaster would be occupied as a Federal post for less than six years. In large part it was a dreary and dull establishment staffed by infantry ill equipped to pursue hostile Indians. The main diversion was escort and patrol duty along a portion of the road from San Antonio to El Paso. The history of the fort was not one of great men and great events. It was more the story of the commonplace life of ordinary soldiers on the isolated frontier of the desert Southwest, during a time when communications relied upon horse and wagon and the road was the vital link to California and the gold fields.

The men who served at Fort Lancaster saw little action and their lives were filled with an unremarkable sameness and monotonous routine. They suffered the isolation of the frontier with each day being much like the one before, with the same companions, the same poor quarters and inadequate rations. There was a greater danger from disease and accidents than from Indians, and army discipline was as harsh as the environment. That these men of the First Infantry lived, and even thrived, under these circumstances makes the history of Fort Lancaster worth telling.

The original research for this project was undertaken for the Interpretative Planning Division of Texas Parks and Wildlife. In the late 1960s five forts were acquired as State Historic Sites. I was working during the summers as a seasonal ranger for the National Park Service at Fort Davis National Historic Site. While attending graduate school at the University of Texas at Austin, I was employed to do research for Parks and Wildlife. I was assigned Fort Lancaster and found it a fascinating project. This interest has continued as time passes. Motivation was added when Dr. Ron Tyler, then at the Amon Carter Museum, provided copies of the two letters written by J. D. B. Stillman from Fort Lancaster in 1855. Stillman, a physician on a transcontinental journey, was appointed temporary medical officer for the post. His comments provided a unique insight into military life on the Texas frontier.

Today Fort Lancaster is maintained as a State Historic Site administered by Texas Parks and Wildlife. Located south of Interstate 10 and just east of Sheffield, it is as removed from civilization now as it was when active. The rare visitor can walk among the ruins undisturbed and, with little imagination, feel the presence of the spirits of the men of the First Regiment of Infantry.

A PRAYER FOR THE DYING
(A Song of the Old Army)

We meet 'neath the sounding rafters,
The walls all around us are bare.
They echo the peals of laughter,
It seems that the dead are there.

So stand by your glasses steady,
This world is a world of lies.
Here's a toast to the dead already;
Hurrah for the next man who dies.

There's a mist on the glass congealing,
'Tis the hurricane's fiery breath.
And thus does the warmth of feeling,
Turn ice in the grip of death.

Oh, stand to your glasses steady,
For a moment the vapor flies.
A cup to the dead already,
An hurrah for the next who dies.

Who dreads to the dust returning?
Who shrinks from the sable shore?
Where the high and haughty yearning,
Of the soul shall sting no more.

So stand to your glasses steady,
'Tis all we have left to prize.
A toast to the dead already,
And hurrah for the next who dies.

Cut off from the land that bore us,
Betrayed by the land we find.
Where the brightest have gone before us,
And the dullest remain behind.

So stand to your glasses steady,
The world is a web of lies.
Then here's to the dead already,
And hurrah for the next man who dies.

Anonymous

3

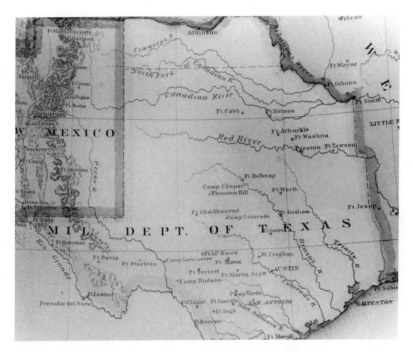

The Military Department of Texas and part of New Mexico. From *Map of the United States, Exhibiting the Military Depts. and Posts*, Quartermaster Department, 1860. *Courtesy author's collection.*

1.
THE ARMY BETWEEN TWO WARS

THE END OF THE MEXICAN WAR and the discovery of gold in California created an overwhelming need for communication with the West. The primary means of transportation and communication, burdensomely slow, were by wagon road. Travel was time consuming, and subject to the vicissitudes of weather. Roads were potentially dangerous, especially where they disrupted the lives and routines of the Native Americans living or hunting in the area. The United States Army was not equipped to deal with the vast area under its jurisdiction. There were not adequate resources to provide even minimal protection for the various established routes west. By establishing posts such as Fort Lancaster at strategic locations, the army attempted to fulfill its assigned mission with limited means.

Fought for the cause of Manifest Destiny, the Mexican War, 1846–1848, together with the Gadsden Purchase, 1853, filled in the southwestern boundaries of the American nation. Before the Mexican War, the United States Army consisted of approximately six thousand men. Charged with protecting the Atlantic Coast, the Great Lakes, and a frontier just west of the Mississippi, this force of regulars consisted primarily of units of infantry and artillery for coastal defense. An invasion force advancing on four major fronts, the army during the Mexican War grew to over forty-seven thousand.

The crucible that would form leaders for both armies in the Civil War, these men were volunteers, mostly, and they quickly mustered out once the conflict ended. However, the postwar mission of the army had changed greatly. With its strength reduced to ten thousand, the army now had to defend a frontier that ranged from the mountains of the Pacific Northwest to the deserts of the Southwest. Of the 166 companies that made up the U.S. Army, the West received 126. While this represented the bulk of available strength, it fell far short of what was actually needed.[1]

The true strength of these various companies was always below that mandated by army regulations. Desertion, discharge, and death produced an annual turnover of 28 percent. This, coupled with the haphazard methods of recruitment, meant that the actual strength of the army consistently fell as much as 18 percent below that authorized by Congress. In 1850, as an attempt to remedy the manpower problem, an Executive Order increased the authorized strength of companies. Enhanced recruitment brought an additional three thousand men into the ranks, but real numbers did not increase significantly beyond ten thousand until 1855. In that year, the demands of frontier defense won out. With the addition of two new infantry and two new cavalry regiments, the army was increased, by Act of Congress, to over fifteen thousand. Even so, company strength fluctuated constantly. The monthly *Post Returns* for Fort Lancaster illustrate the situation. In January 1856 both companies manning the post mustered only eighty-nine soldiers between them, but by February strength was up to seventy apiece.[2]

Fort Lancaster illustrated another major weakness of the U.S. Army in this period. For the duration of its existence, infantry garrisoned the fort. The military leadership understood that the most effective way to patrol the roads and fight the nomadic Indian tribes was with mounted troops. However, only Congress had the authority to establish the composition of the army, and cavalry cost more than infantry. Consequently the greater number of regiments were infantry. J. D. B. Stillman, a civilian doctor serving under contract at Fort Lancaster in 1855, clearly described the problem: "what can be expected when an officer is sent with a company of riflemen, when they are sent with a long train of wagons, which can . . . barely carry forage for their own mules' consumption, thundering over the road, encumbered with hen coops and milch cows, tents, heavy bedding and all the paraphernalia of the camps of a regular army, and their progress announced with a flourish of trumpets."[3]

On the national level there was no coherent Indian policy. Various administrations approached the problem differently, leaving the army without clear direction. Even without a policy, there was no lack of national debate. There were three general concepts regularly argued: subjugation, removal to reservations, and acculturation. With no consistent direction and large numbers of people moving west, the army developed a network of small posts protecting strategic areas.[4]

The Quartermaster Department estimated that it cost between $250,000 and $300,000 per year to maintain an infantry regiment in garrison; the estimate for mounted units was twice as high. To keep cavalry in the field for a year was estimated to cost $1,500,000. And these figures did not include the initial costs of forming the regiment and supplying it with horses. These costs discouraged Congress from allocating the funds for the necessary mounted units, so it fell largely to the infantry to protect the frontier from highly mobile Indians. Thus, with the bulk of the army being infantry, and inadequate to the task at hand, experiments in mounting foot soldiers were conducted. They were only partially successful for, as Gen. Winfield Scott wrote, mounting foot soldiers "can only result in disorganizing the infantry, and converting them into extremely indifferent horsemen."[5]

Fundamentally, the army was underfunded and ill-used. Part of this was a result of its own disorganization, and the lack of an effective command structure. Seldom was policy or strategy initiated in the War Department or U.S. Army Headquarters in Washington. Headquarters was often limited to ratifying decisions made by commanders in the field, and its time was largely spent in the unending task of procuring men and supplies and shipping them to the points of greatest need on the frontier.

Power and authority within the War Department and U.S. Army was diffused and decentralized. The secretary of war held

U.S. Army uniforms, General-in-Chief, Engineers, Artillery, and Military Academy Cadets, 1858–1861. H. A. Ogden, *Uniforms of the United States Army. Photograph courtesy Fort Davis National Historic Site.*

most of the power, while the general in chief was primarily a figurehead. The heads of the staff departments, the adjutant general, quartermaster general, surgeon general, and chief engineer, did not report to the army commander. All reported directly to the secretary of war. As a result, each operated independently, with the strongest department being the adjutant general, the keeper of records and the dispenser of orders. This situation often brought the commanding general into conflict with the secretary of war. Gen. Winfield Scott, the army commander through the 1850s, was in constant conflict with the secretary of war, Jefferson Davis.[6]

The general in chief also suffered from being too far removed from the field, and was unable to exert effective control over his line officers. Without direction from Washington, the commanders of the various geographic departments shaped frontier defense policy. At the time Fort Lancaster was established, the Department of Texas was under the command of Bvt. Maj. Gen. Persifor F. Smith, who was responsible for the defense of the region.

While the adjutant general was the most powerful, the Quartermaster Department had the greatest influence on the men in the field. In 1848 this department primarily supplied eastern garrisons, most of which were readily accessible, but by 1855 there were more than fifty forts scattered over two million square miles. The Quartermaster Department had to contract with civilian freighters, and see to it that the troops in the field were supplied with an unending procession of salt beef, salt pork, bread, coffee, and a variety of other necessities. This often proved to be an impossible task.[7]

With a decentralized command structure, much depended upon the quality of the officers in the field. It was from these ranks that both the North and the South would draw their military leadership during the Civil War, and the success and fame of some of these men attest to the overall quality of officers. However, the officers corps demonstrated contrasts ranging from energy, competence, and youth, to lethargy, incompetence, and age. The two greatest internal problems were slow promotion and low pay, both of which prompted many resignations. Pay ranged from twenty-five dollars per month for lieutenants to seventy-five dollars per month for colonels. Even considering allowances for rations, quarters, servants, fuel, and forage, this was far below what could be earned as a civilian. In 1857 Congress did raise the base pay by twenty dollars per month.[8]

For many the promotion rate was more discouraging than the low pay. Officers advanced strictly by seniority—through captain in the regiment, through colonel in the infantry or artillery corps, and through the higher ranks in the army at large. There was no retirement list, which made promotion agonizingly slow, as officers were often kept on the rolls long after their effectiveness was gone. Junior officers were kept from the field grades until past their prime, taking twenty to thirty years to reach the rank of major. J. D. B. Stillman, writing from Fort Lancaster in 1855, describes the plight of junior officers as follows, "during the lone night while he listens to the sentry's call, and the wolf's answer from the hill, what has he to think of but the chances of his promotion, or orders to some new post, which he hopes will at least afford him a change, if it does not improve his situation. He has superiors." He then adds, "I do not know that I would not read the announcement of the demise of old Maj. Longwind, whereby I add a new bar to my shoulder-strap, with more unacknowledged satisfaction than I would of sorrow at the death of my junior officer."[9]

Compounding the problem was the use of brevet promotion to reward battlefield achievement. Indian fights did not qualify, but most of the veteran officers of the Mexican War held one or more brevets. Many lieutenants and captains held brevets of major or colonel, while more than half of the colonels in the army held brevets of brigadier or major general. If these awards had been only honorary, there would have been no problem. However, under certain circumstances, they took effect in both rank and pay. Brevet ranks applied in commands composed of different corps, in detachments constituted of different corps, on courts-martial, and by designation of the president. This resulted in endless confusion.[10]

The officer corps was anything but a tight band of professional soldiers. Factions were constantly quarreling: infantry against cavalry, staff against line, and—the sectionalism of the day being reflected strongly in the military—North against South.[11] By the 1850s, 70 percent of officers possessed a West Point education, though there was no guarantee in this that a man would be a good officer. The Academy functioned primarily as an engineering college, but did serve to instill a sense of pride in its graduates; when it came to the challenges of protecting the frontier and fighting hostile Indians, however, even those educated at West Point were on their own.

In the field the army was organized into regiments of ten companies each. The artillery was divided into twelve companies, but ten of these functioned as infantry. After the reorganization of 1855, there were ten regiments of infantry, four of artillery, and five of mounted troops. The five mounted regiments were of three types: two of cavalry, two of dragoons, and one of mounted rifles, the latter being essentially a regiment of mounted infantry.

Each regimental company was under the command of a captain, assisted by a first and a second lieutenant and an orderly sergeant. Each company consisted of four squads with a sergeant and a corporal. The regimental field and staff consisted of a colonel, a lieutenant colonel, two majors and an adjutant. A quartermaster was detailed from the line officers. A sergeant major, quartermaster sergeant, and musician composed the noncommissioned staff. A regiment theoretically numbered nine hundred, but in reality one or two officers and forty men per company was the average. The monthly *Post Returns* from Fort Lancaster show company strength fluctuating from forty to eighty men.[12]

The fort was the central institution of the frontier army. All forts conformed to a basic pattern; most were isolated far from settlements, and were built with the materials at hand. In the Southwest this meant a liberal use of earth for construction. Where available, thatch, canvas, stone, and wood were also relied upon. Construction was a continuing process as a post progressed from rude temporary structures to permanent buildings. The first shelters at Camp Lancaster were of the most temporary construction, but by the time of abandonment the garrison had erected permanent stone and adobe buildings.

The fort was a self-contained community with its own official and social life based upon military rank and routine. There were families at even the most isolated posts. At the top of a strict hierarchy were the commanding officer and his wife, while at the bottom were the enlisted families. Between the officers and enlisted personnel there was little interaction, but each group managed to create its own social life. The post adjutant and sergeant major

U.S. Army uniforms, Artillery, Infantry, Mounted Rifles, Light Artillery, 1855–1858. H. A. Ogden, *Uniforms of the United States Army. Photograph courtesy Fort Davis National Historic Site.*

were the administrative agents of the commanding officer. The post quartermaster was responsible for supplying and housing the garrison, and the commissary officer was responsible for feeding it. A surgeon, often a civilian under government contract, operated the hospital and watched over the sanitary conditions of the post. Company officers and noncommissioned officers supervised their units, and, working at their respective tasks, were the enlisted specialists: blacksmith, carpenter, cobbler, and baker. Drum or bugle calls regulated the routine of the day.[13]

U.S. Army uniforms, Cavalry and Dragoons, 1855–1858. H. A. Ogden, *Uniforms of the United States Army. Photograph courtesy Fort Davis National Historic Site.*

Garrison duty was the main occupation on the frontier. This consisted of a monotonous routine of drill, guard duty, and the unending construction and repair of the fort, called "fatigue duty." There were escorts and scout patrols to break the routine, and there was leisure time, but few ways to enjoy it. The soldier was forced to create his own forms of amusement, and he produced a wide variety. Reading was important to many, and at posts such as Fort Lancaster hunting and fishing were popular diversions that added variety to the common fare of the mess hall. However, the main entertainment was often drinking and gambling. Gambling was officially prohibited, but most soldiers readily participated and freely parted with their pay. The army attempted to control the use of alcohol, but it was never eliminated. At Fort Lancaster the two main sources of alcohol were the civilian sutler and travelers along the road.

For an enlisted man the army offered little. A recruit joined for five years and after 1854, when there was a pay raise, he earned eleven dollars a month in the infantry and artillery and twelve dollars a month in the mounted regiments. If a man made sergeant he could look forward to seventeen dollars a month, but even this was less than a civilian laborer could make. To encourage re-enlistment there was an additional two dollars a month for the second hitch, and one dollar a month for each thereafter. The paymaster was to visit each post every two months, but it was not unusual for an isolated garrison to go without pay for as long as six months. Army life mostly involved common labor rather than the pursuit of hostile Indians. The lack of civilian labor at most frontier locations, and the need to economize meant that the enlisted soldier had to do the work of construction and maintenance. Still, the army did manage to attract recruits despite the hardship, isolation, and low pay. Many were immigrants unable to find other work, while some were men lured west for adventure. Many were running from the law. The ideal recruit, as far as the army was concerned, was the stereotypical American farm boy, but not many of these joined the ranks. Immigrants, mostly Irish and German, filled out the enlisted ranks.[14]

When a recruit joined the army he received his uniform, rations, and weapons, and was provided with quarters. The daily ration varied as little as the daily routine. At many locations, in order to vary the diet, a post garden was maintained. The inspector general of the army, Col. Joseph Mansfield, in his inspection of Fort Lancaster in 1860, wrote that the commanding officer, Capt. Robert Granger, "has repeatedly made efforts for a post garden; and the past season by great labor, has succeeded in supplying his men with mellons, and Summer vegetables to a considerable extent. But all the plants have to be watered by hand."[15]

The uniform of the day was no more adequate than the rations. According to regulations the men should have been well clothed. However, as in other areas, theory was not up to practice. The full uniform consisted of a double-breasted frock coat, long pants, ankle-length boots, and a hat with pompons. The uniforms were dark blue with different facings to denote the various service branches: orange for dragoons, yellow for cavalry, green for the Regiment of Mounted Rifles, scarlet for artillery, and sky blue for infantry. Poorly made under government contract, the uniform usually had to be modified to fit, and no consideration was given to the various environmental conditions on the frontier. Whether in the deserts of the Southwest or the snows of the Northwest, the uniform was the same.[16]

In a period of rapidly advancing technology, army weapons did not always keep pace with change, especially on the frontier. In his 1856 inspection of the fort, Inspector General Mansfield found both companies still armed with muskets rather than the new rifled musket issued in 1855. Luckily, the army did manage to arm its soldiers with better weapons than those generally possessed by the Indians. The years between the Mexican War and the Civil War saw the development of the percussion cap, revolving pistols, rifles that replaced muskets, and breech loading mechanisms. Although the Ordnance Department did not change as fast as weapons technology, the soldiers did benefit some. Until 1855, the infantry was armed with the .69 caliber smoothbore musket adopted in 1842. In 1855 the Ordnance Department began to issue the new rifle and rifled musket, Model 1855. These new weapons used an elongated, expanding bullet, and were .58 caliber. They had long-range sights and attachments for the twenty-two-and-one-half-inch saber-bayonet.[17]

Although supplied with arms, no system of basic training prepared recruits as soldiers. Men enlisting on the frontier did so at the various department headquarters. Those enlisting in the East chose one of three induction centers: infantry went to Governor's Island, New York; cavalry to Carlisle Barracks, Pennsylvania; and

U.S. Army uniforms, Staff, Field, Line Officers, and Enlisted Men, 1858–1861. H. A. Ogden, *Uniforms of the United States Army. Photograph courtesy Fort Davis National Historic Site.*

artillery to Newport Barracks, Kentucky. Since the demand for replacements was great, men were sent to their regiments with little or no training. It was left to the company officers and noncommissioned officers to provide instruction. Due to the usual lack of line officers at the individual frontier posts and the amount of time spent on fatigue duty, a recruit learned his trade more from experience than from formal training.

Actual contact with hostile Indians in the field was relatively uncommon. From 1849 to 1861 the army fought eighty-four engagements in Texas. Fifty-three of these occurred during the years Fort Lancaster was active. Many of these were the result of the arrival in Texas of the Second Cavalry. The First Infantry, scattered in small garrisons like Fort Lancaster throughout frontier Texas, was engaged only fourteen times between 1849 and 1861. Most of these were small unit actions between patrols of twenty-five or fewer and Indian raiding parties of fewer than twenty.[18]

Tactics were mostly reactive with pursuit being the most common operation. Word would be received of a raid, and troops would be dispatched from the closest garrison. Other than pursuit, the most prevalent form of contact came through patrols. Regular patrols were common along the roads, along major streams, at river fords, and at favorite waterholes. A deliberate attack by a large force, with detailed planning and coordination by either the army or the Indians, was uncommon. In general, contact was serendipitous, and the fight brief. After a few casualties the Indians would retreat, and the army seldom pursued. It was more than possible for a soldier, especially an infantryman, to go through an entire enlistment without experiencing a combat situation. It is likely that some of the troops at Fort Lancaster never encountered a hostile Indian.[19]

The likelihood of dying in action was actually much less than death from disease or accident. The *Post Returns* from Fort Lancaster list a total of 285 cases of illness in less than six years, with the record being eighteen men reported in hospital during the month of May 1858. On average each soldier in the army was hospitalized three times a year. Respiratory ailments, various fevers, exposure to the elements, and venereal disease were the common illnesses. To handle medical needs on the frontier was a greatly undermanned staff of physicians and assistants, who nevertheless managed to keep the death rate down to that comparable to the army in the East. The staff of trained army physicians on the frontier rarely exceeded one hundred, their number supplemented by physicians employed on contract. During its existence Fort Lancaster was never without the services of a doctor for any length of time. However, the hospital was never the most modern structure at the post. Originally it was a *jacal*, a structure of vertical pickets and a thatched roof. By 1860, when inspected by General Mansfield, the hospital was "a very poor adobe building, braced on one end."[20]

Considering the hardships, privations, dull routine, and lack of diversion, it is understandable that desertion and discipline were major problems. Nearly three thousand men deserted each year, and in 1855, when the army was increased to 15,000 soldiers, 3,233 deserted. By 1860 the overall desertion rate was down to 12 percent. Discipline problems also took their toll. According to the *Post Returns*, Fort Lancaster had an average of seven men in the guardhouse each month, with a record twenty-three confined in May 1857. The Articles of War left most punishment up to the officers of a court-martial, which provided a wide range of possibilities. For minor offenses solitary confinement on bread and water, or forfeiture of pay and allowances were normal sentences. The more brutal punishments were saved for deserters. The Articles of War allowed for a sentence of death, but in practice flogging and branding were used. The procedure was fifty lashes, "well laid on," and the letter "D" branded on the hip. In this manner a man was drummed out of the service.[21]

With few exceptions there is no mention of women and children in association with Fort Lancaster. This is not an uncommon situation at frontier garrisons. Most soldiers were unmarried, often not by choice but by circumstance. At some posts Indian and Mexican women, as well as prostitutes, were accessible. However, no settlement or encampment grew up around Fort Lancaster.[22]

Except for laundresses, army regulations took no official recognition of women, including the wives and families of officers. Each post needed laundresses, and regulations called for one for each seventeen men, with no more than four per company. Each was accorded rations and bedding. Most, if not all, were wives of enlisted personnel, and they depended upon the good will of the post commander for quarters. In his inspection of 1857, Mansfield listed five laundresses, and in 1860 he listed four quarters for laundresses.[23]

Even for the wives of officers conditions on the frontier were crude. Personal items and furniture were limited to what could be hauled by wagon. Basic food staples came from the commissary, and were plain at best. Depending upon the location game, fish, and fresh vegetables might be available. Fort Lancaster had a garden, but, as mentioned earlier, watering it was laborious.[24]

Usually children were present but few records exist. Lt. John Sherburne brought his wife and child to Fort Lancaster in 1857. While stationed there, a second child was born. The only other record is the death of Capt. Arthur Lee's fifteen-month-old son, who died at Fort Lancaster on July 9, 1857, as the family prepared to return to Fort Davis. Regardless of the lack of documentation, any children at the post would undoubtedly have been the center of attention.[25]

The period between the Mexican War and the Civil War was one of transition for the U.S. Army. Faced with the tasks of protecting a rapidly expanding frontier and developing new strategic policies, and handicapped by fragmented leadership and a decentralized command structure, the army did its best with limited resources. Poorly supplied, equipped, and housed, the frontier soldiers did manage to perform their primary tasks: to survey and protect the roads that united the continent.

2.
WAGON ROADS WEST

WITH THE DISCOVERY OF GOLD in California the need for communication and a continental transportation network became paramount. This was so pressing that unique experiments, such as the Pony Express and the use of camels, were undertaken. The period between the Mexican War and the Civil War would be one of intense, scientific exploration of the American West. The goals were to establish a transcontinental transportation network, and to delineate the United States boundaries with Mexico and Canada. The army took the lead both in keeping the lines of communication open, and in exploration. Fort Lancaster was established to protect a major route to California.

Although the Spanish, having explored the Rio Grande and Pecos Rivers for most of their courses, were familiar with West Texas, at the beginning of the republic period the maps of this part of Texas were still devoid of detail; and, though there was great desire to take some of the Santa Fe trade away from Missouri, the Republic of Texas did nothing with its western domain. The Missouri merchants controlled the main supply route to Santa Fe, and with this monopoly they, in effect, also controlled the lucrative Chihuahua City trade as well. In an attempt to shorten the Missouri to Chihuahua City route, the first effort to explore West Texas in the republic period was lead by Dr. Henry Connally, a Missouri trader. In 1839–1840, leading a party of Texans and Mexicans, Connally

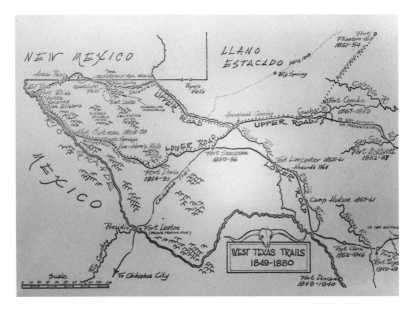

West Texas Trails. By Jerry Harlan. *Courtesy Jerry Harlan.*

crossed the Red River and journeyed through Central Texas to
Horsehead Crossing on the Pecos. From there he proceeded via
Comanche Springs (Fort Stockton) to Paisano Pass (Alpine), then
down Alamito Creek to La Junta, the junction of the Rio Conchos
and Rio Grande (near present-day Presidio), and from there to
Chihuahua City. Ten years later, this route became part of the major trading route from San Antonio.[26]

No other formal survey was undertaken until after the Mexican
War. The war itself generated much interest and information
about the Southwest. The key to the American victory was the military leadership in the four primary theaters of operation. Gen.
Zachary Taylor invaded Mexico from the mouth of the Rio
Grande, fighting key battles at Monterrey and Buena Vista and se-
curing the boundary of Texas. Gen. Stephen Watts Kearney invaded New Mexico and captured, without firing a shot, the important
trade center of Santa Fe. From there he marched overland, and
with Lt. John C. Fremont and Commodore Robert Stockton, was

instrumental in taking California for the Union. Gen. Winfield Scott made an amphibious landing at Vera Cruz, fought his way overland, and captured Mexico City. With the Treaty of Guadalupe Hidalgo in 1848 and the Gadsden Purchase in 1853, Mexico ceded the entire Southwest. In 1848 gold was discovered in California. The necessity for roads to connect the East with California and the effort to establish an exact boundary with Mexico touched off a flurry of exploration.

The need for an all-weather route to California, the desire to tap the lucrative trade with northern Mexico through Chihuahua City, and the budding national interest in a transcontinental railroad route stimulated the exploration of West Texas. There were several allies aiding this endeavor. The first two were the powerful senators from Texas, Sam Houston and Thomas Rusk. Soon after statehood they both called for a transcontinental survey through Texas, and advocated a railroad through the state, to terminate in California. Above all they were ready and willing to call upon Washington to administer to the needs of Texas. The other primary assistance came from the Army Corps of Topographical Engineers. Commanded in Washington by Col. John James Abert, the corps was responsible for Federal road, coast, and resource surveys. Some of the best officers in the corps were stationed in Texas, under the local command of Bvt. Lt. Col. Joseph E. Johnston. His various subordinates included Lieutenants William H. C. Whiting, William F. Smith, Francis Bryan, and Nathaniel Michler.[27]

In 1848 commercial interests in San Antonio raised eight hundred dollars, and enlisted John Coffee Hays to find a practical route to El Paso. Hays was escorted by a contingent of Texas Rangers under the command of Capt. Samuel Highsmith. The party of thirty-seven left San Antonio on August 27, and returned three and a half months later, after encountering great difficulty. Close to starvation, the expedition had made it only as far as Presidio, making no attempt to reach El Paso. Trying to traverse the harsh Big Bend country, both Hays and Highsmith reported that they had found a trail. In reality this survey accomplished little. By the time Hays and Highsmith returned to San Antonio, the news of the discovery of gold in California had reached the East.

A southern all-weather route across the continent then became an imperative. As 1849 dawned, gold seekers began to arrive at the major population centers of Texas, ready to leave at the first opportunity. When cholera broke out, many started west before the end of winter, and before a satisfactory trail had been surveyed.[28]

Understanding the immediacy of the problem, Bvt. Maj. Gen. William Worth, the commanding officer in Texas, ordered Lt. William H. C. Whiting and Lt. William F. Smith to find a suitable route to El Paso. Departing from San Antonio on February 9, 1849, they were instructed to follow the Hays-Highsmith trail as far as Presidio, and then to continue up the Rio Grande to El Paso. They were instructed that if this route was not feasible they were to find a more practical way home. By February 21 they were at the frontier of settlement. Whiting wrote, "at an hour late in the afternoon my party left Fredericksburg, the last settlement it was to see until Presidio del Norte should be reached. This little town is a colony of the Dutch, many of whom have emigrated to Texas and pushed their settlements in every direction. It has a pretty site on Barrons creek, one of the little streams that swell the Perdernales, and some day or other may become a place of importance, but now its people are miserably poor." Here they were able to add to their numbers. "Captain Eastman, First Infantry, is encamped near this place, and to his polite assistance I am much indebted in increasing my scanty outfit. Here I employed another man, William Howard; he had been out with Hays. We now number sixteen, including Lieutenant Smith, Dick Howard, the two Mexicans, my servant, and myself."[29]

Crossing the San Saba near Fredericksburg, the expedition went three days without water before reaching Live Oak Creek near the Pecos River. Here the party camped in the vicinity of the future location of Fort Lancaster. Describing the area in his journal, Whiting wrote, "this little stream of limpid water, called Live Oak creek from the growth near its mouth, makes its way to the Pecos through a ravine, or canyon, remarkable for its striking formation—a basin enclosed by a general ridge, with detached peaks or spurs resting against its elevation in the form of truncated cones. They are marked by two distinct, horizontal beds of limestone at different heights. These appear at the sides of the hills and look, in their regularity, like walls of masonry, the upper one bounding the top. The summits are level and apparently at the same general elevation of the great table prairie, out of which they seem to have been cut by the same great aqueous convulsion."[30] The expedition found the area laced by Indian trails. Due to the exhausted condition of their animals, they remained in camp for a day.

Traveling through the Davis Mountains to Presidio, the expedition then followed the Rio Grande to El Paso. This outbound route was unsatisfactory, so hoping to find a better trail and especially one with more water, they returned by following the Rio Grande for only the first hundred miles. At that point they marched due east for the Pecos. Following the river south for sixty miles they crossed to the Devil's River, proceeded to its junction with the Rio Grande, and then east to San Antonio via Fort Clark. Whiting and Smith reported that their return route was satisfactory. It would soon be one of two major routes west through Texas.

While Whiting and Smith were in the field, another expedition was formed as a cooperative venture between commercial interests in Austin and the military. Austin merchants raised the funds necessary to send John S. Ford to seek a route to El Paso, and General Worth sent Maj. Robert Neighbors to represent the military and federal interests. Neighbors was the federal Indian agent for Texas, and Ford, a former Texas Ranger, was publisher of the *Texas Democrat* in Austin. This party left Austin in March 1849 heading northward along the Colorado River to Brady's Creek, a tributary of the San Saba River. Striking west to the Concho River and Horsehead Crossing on the Pecos, they traversed the stark desert north of the Davis Mountains to El Paso. Not finding enough water to make this a practical road, the expedition returned by a more northerly route. Leaving El Paso they followed the general course of the present Texas-New Mexico border through the Guadalupe Mountains to the Pecos. Moving south down the river to Horsehead Crossing, they returned to Austin via Fredericksburg and San Antonio. Ford and Neighbors reported that the return route, with only minor improvements, would make an excellent wagon road.[31]

General Worth died of cholera on May 7, 1849. His successor was Bvt. Brig. Gen. William S. Harney. Even before the Whiting-Smith and Ford-Neighbors expeditions returned, he had plans for a further survey of the two possible roads. Harney was more interested in the southern route and assigned Lt. Col. Joseph Johnston to the survey. Returning with Whiting just as Johnston was leaving, Smith was ordered to immediately turn around and accompany Johnston. Johnston's party of engineers, escorted by a company of the First Infantry, was to proceed in conjunction with Maj. Jefferson Van Horne and his six companies of Third Infantry on their way to El Paso to establish a garrison there. Also accompanying the expedition was a party of California bound immigrants. The Topographical Engineers surveyed ahead of the main column, and Capt. Samuel G. French of the Quartermaster Department commanded a detail assigned to make the necessary road improvements. They arrived without incident at El Paso on September 3, having made only small changes to Whiting and Smith's original route. This trail would be known as the Lower, or Military, Road.[32]

Harney assigned Lt. Francis T. Bryan to survey the northern route of Ford and Neighbors. On June 14, 1849, Bryan departed San Antonio westward to the Pecos. The party found easy passage all the way to El Paso, which was reached on July 29. The major problem with this potential road was a lack of water between the Concho and Pecos Rivers. In his report Bryan suggested the possibility of digging wells in this area. Once in El Paso, Bryan joined Johnston, and in October both officers and their men returned to San Antonio by this northern route. By this time a trail was well established, and soon to be known as the Upper Road. The final connection for the network of western roads across Texas was the establishment of a route from Fort Smith, Arkansas, that joined the Upper Road at the Pecos River. Capt. Randolph Marcy of the Fifth Infantry and Lt. Nathaniel Michler were responsible for this survey.[33]

Before the official surveys were complete, the Lower and Upper Roads were in use by gold-seekers on their way to California. Over three thousand *argonauts* left from Texas in 1849, with many going by way of northern Mexico. Others followed the surveyors,

Camp in Snow Storm on Delaware Creek, Texas. From John Russell Bartlett, *Personal Narrative of Explorations and Incidents in Texas, New Mexico, California, Sonora, and Chihuahua, Connected with the United States Boundary Commission, 1850–1853* (New York, 1854). Bartlett's Boundary Commission was one of the first groups to use the Upper Road. *Photograph courtesy author's collection.*

or attached themselves to military columns such as that of Johnston and Van Horne. Emigrants starting for the gold fields from Fort Smith or Dallas used the Upper Road. The Lower Road was used by those booking sea passage to the ports on the Gulf of Mexico, and then traveling overland to San Antonio. The Lower Road also came into prominence as an alternative trade route to Chihuahua City.

The Chihuahua Trail, longer than the Santa Fe Trail, had the advantage of a port terminal on the Gulf of Mexico at Indianola on Matagorda Bay. The trail passed through San Antonio, where it joined the Lower Road as far as Comanche Springs (Fort Stockton), and then headed south to Presidio and Chihuahua City. More difficult than the Santa Fe Trail, this was still a profitable route for those strong enough to survive the hardships. Two hundred companies were engaged at the height of trade. Business along the Chihuahua City Trail was interrupted by the Civil War, but survived until the coming of the railroads.[34]

The Lower, or Military, Road was the army's primary supply

route west to El Paso and Fort Bliss. In 1850 the largest supply train ever to use this road gathered at Fort Inge near Uvalde. Bound for El Paso and consisting of 340 loaded wagons, 450 civilians, and 175 soldiers, the expedition was under the command of Bvt. Maj. John Sprague. Four thousand animals including cattle, mules, oxen, and horses accompanied the wagons. To conserve water and forage the train was divided into two divisions. Sprague's mission was to supply the garrison at El Paso and escort civilian merchants, as well as protect gold-seekers rushing to California.[35]

Accompanying the military escort was Lt. Parmenas T. Turnley of the First Infantry. Although Turnley's company would be part of the garrison that established Fort Lancaster, he was by then on detached duty, and was promoted out of the regiment before he could return to Texas. Turnley was an engineer of some skill. He developed a prefabricated building system that would be used at Fort Lancaster. As the expedition's quartermaster and commissary officer, he also had on hand the materials to build a simple iron bridge across the Pecos River near Live Oak Creek, close by the future site of Fort Lancaster. At best, this bridge was designed to be temporary and was initially poorly constructed. The normal crossing was a nearby ford.[36]

The establishment of the Upper and Lower Roads did not end the exploration of the Trans-Pecos. In 1850 the United States Boundary Commissioner, John Russell Bartlett, used the Upper Road to travel to El Paso to meet his Mexican counterpart, Gen. Pedro García Conde; and in 1851 the boundary commissioner and Maj. William H. Emory of the Topographical Engineers surveyed the Big Bend-Presidio area.[37]

In 1853, Congress authorized the Pacific Railway Surveys, the first great scientific exploration of the West. One of those surveys would be conducted along the Thirty-second Parallel in proximity to the Upper Road. It was understood that, with limited national resources, there would be only one subsidized railroad route to the Pacific. However, as a result of sectionalism the selection of a route was one of the most complicated political problems of the period. Both the North and the South expected this road to have its eastern terminus in their region.

Congress authorized what was thought to be the final solution to the problem. The War Department, under Secretary Jefferson Davis, was to survey all of the principle routes, and decide, objectively, which was most economical and practical. Four main parties, and several secondary groups, were sent into the field. Initially under the command of Maj. William Emory, and then under Capt. Andrew Atkinson, most of the officers were from the Corps of Topographical Engineers. While all of this activity was intended to unravel the political knots of selecting a transcontinental route, it was not to be. After a year's work and a published report in twelve volumes, the surveyors found that there were several practical routes, four of which were economically viable. Of these four, two would have a terminus in the North and two in the South. The chance for a nonpolitical resolution died in 1854. It would be ten more years before a solution could be found and then only after the South withdrew from the debate by seceding from the Union.[38]

In October 1853, as one of the four major surveys, Lt. John Pope was ordered to find a possible route along and near the Thirty-second Parallel from Doña Ana, above El Paso, to Preston on the Red River. Lt. John G. Parke was to make the survey from California to Doña Ana. Not starting until February 1854, Pope had two main tasks. The first was to find a suitable pass through the Guadalupe Mountains, and the second was to seek out sources of water on the Llano Estacado. Since most of the route was already known through the work of Bryan, Marcy, and Michler, Pope encountered few problems. With the provision that artesian wells could be developed to provide water, he found a route acceptable for a railroad. The next year Pope was sent back to the Staked Plains to dig wells. He made several attempts, but his equipment was inadequate and the mission was deemed a failure.[39]

There was no railroad survey of the Lower Road, which in many ways was an excellent choice for a route. During the 1880s, the Southern Pacific used this for the most southern of several transcontinental railroads. In the meantime one of the more unusual transportation experiments ever conducted by the United States Army was undertaken through West Texas.

Encampment of 6th June, a typical army survey party, consisting of engineers, surveyors, scientists, artists, and an escort for protection. This scene is from the Texas Panhandle on the North Fork of the Red River. From Capt. Randolph Marcy, *Exploration of the Red River of Louisiana in the year 1852* (Washington, 1853). *Photograph courtesy author's collection.*

In 1855, Secretary of War Jefferson Davis urged Congress to appropriate funds for the purchase of camels in order to conduct experiments in the desert Southwest. There was an initial appropriation of thirty thousand dollars. On May 14, 1856, thirty-three camels, three Arabs, and two Turks landed at Indianola. On February 10, 1857, forty-one more camels arrived. The permanent base for these animals was Camp Verde, sixty miles northwest of San Antonio. The first assignment of this unusual contingent was to survey a wagon road from Fort Defiance, New Mexico, to the Colorado River. Under the command of Lt. Edward Beale of the U.S. Navy, the camels used the Lower Road, stopping at Fort Lancaster.

In May 1859, Lt. William Echols was ordered to test the practicality of the camels by finding a shorter route through the Trans-Pecos to Fort Davis. The expedition included an escort under Lt. Edward Hartz. With twenty-four mules and twenty-four camels,

Echols surveyed much of the Big Bend country. He reported that the camels performed well, while many of the mules died due to the lack of water. In 1860, Echols was asked to repeat his effort. Over rougher terrain he was to find a direct trail from the Pecos River to Fort Davis. At one point the expedition was without water for a period of five days, with the camels saving the command. Although they demonstrated their worth, the camels were not used again. The Civil War ended the experiments and the herd at Camp Verde was dispersed.[40]

Both the Upper and Lower Roads served as overland mail routes. In September 1851, Henry Skillman received a government contract to carry the mail from San Antonio to El Paso and Santa Fe. Operations began in San Antonio on November 3, and the first mail was delivered to Santa Fe on November 24. By December of that year, Skillman was offering passenger service. In October 1854, Skillman joined in partnership with George H. Giddings, a San Antonio merchant. Giddings soon became the major force in this endeavor.

At first mules carried the mail, but in order to transport passengers the partners soon converted to wagons. The mail usually consisted of one or two wagons with an armed escort. In 1857, John Birch won a contract to carry the mail from San Antonio to San Diego on a semimonthly schedule. Pooling his stock with Birch, George Giddings signed on as the agent for the eastern division. Giddings continued to operate independently between San Antonio and Santa Fe. Regardless of ownership and contracts, Indian attacks along the route and at the various stations were incessant, including raids at the Fort Lancaster station in December 1857, and April 1858.[41]

On March 3, 1857, a bill passed Congress that would authorize a subsidy for an overland mail contract to San Francisco. In September, John Butterfield and his associates won the contract for twice-weekly service with a subsidy of six hundred thousand dollars. The mail would go from St. Louis to Fort Smith, El Paso, Yuma, Los Angeles, and San Francisco. This southern route was bitterly criticized, but the decision stood. The Butterfield Overland Mail went into operation in September 1858. Initially there were 141 stations. These soon increased to over two hundred. Originally the route followed the Upper Road through Texas. However, on August 1, 1859, the Post Office Department ordered the service changed to the Lower Road from the Pecos River to El Paso, as this route provided more water, and Forts Lancaster, Stockton, Davis, Quitman, and Bliss provided protection.[42]

For the mail and the many parties of emigrants to arrive safely in California, the roads had to be secured. With a small army, primarily of foot soldiers, there were few options open to the military command. Under the circumstances the only viable method was to concentrate on protecting the roads. Neither infantry on foot, mounted on mules, or in wagons were effective off the beaten path. In the rugged terrain of West Texas, regular mounted troops were not much more capable, especially on long marches where water and forage were sparse.[43]

Patrolling the roads was a cumbersome, and not particularly effective task. When patrols were sent in search of hostile Indians, contact was more serendipitous than planned. The only feasible solution in the grand scheme was to build forts within reasonable distance of each other and guard the roads. "Reasonable distance" was always dictated by the need for shelter and water. Both were available along Live Oak Creek on the Lower Road between Fort Clark and Fort Davis.

3.
CAMP LANCASTER

BY 1855 THE LOWER ROAD TO EL PASO was well established, but, with no military presence between Fort Clark and Fort Davis, protection was inadequate. To partially fill this gap, Bvt. Maj. Gen. Persifor Smith, commanding the Department of Texas, determined to build a new post near where the Lower Road crossed the Pecos River. Smith traveled extensively throughout his command and personally selected the sites for several of the forts in Texas, including Fort Davis. While not known for sure, it is conceivable that he chose the location for Fort Lancaster. Capt. Stephen Carpenter, the officer who founded the post, suggested the name Lancaster. Carpenter and Job Roberts Hamilton Lancaster were classmates at West Point, and they had been commissioned together as second lieutenants in the First Infantry on July 1, 1840. Lancaster, seventh in his class at the Military Academy, was killed by lightning on July 5, 1841.[44]

On July 20, 1855, General Smith issued Special Orders No. 79. This order stated that, "as soon as the necessary transportation is provided, the two companies of the 1st Infantry designated to occupy the camp on the El Paso road, pursuant to Special Orders No. 60, Current Series, will proceed to and establish their camp at or near the crossing of Live Oak Creek. . . ." Captain Carpenter was authorized to employ a civilian physician, "there being at present no Medical Officer available." On August 7, Captain Carpenter and

106 men of Companies H and K of the First Infantry marched from Fort Duncan to establish Camp Lancaster at the pre-selected site on Live Oak Creek. Covering 225 miles, the command reached their post on August 20. Upon arrival, H Company mustered fifty-one men, and K Company mustered fifty-three, two of whom were ill. Six men of the command were under arrest.[45]

The only officers with Carpenter were 2nd Lts. Samuel Reynolds and George Williams. First Lt. Charles Underwood of H Company died of an undefined illness the day before the column left Fort Duncan. Marching with Carpenter's command were 104 men of the Eighth Infantry, replacements for Fort Davis. Carpenter wrote in his monthly report, "this Det[achment] consisting of Cos. H&K, 1 Inf. and 108 Recruits and men for the 8th and 1 Prvt. for the 3rd Inf. left Fort Duncan Tex. the 7th, and arrived at this place 'Camp Lancaster' on live oak creek the 20th Aug. 1855. Said Camp is about 1/2 mile above the junction of said ck." General Smith instructed the replacement column for Fort Davis that, "the tents and means of transportation forwarded with the detachment of recruits for the 8th Infantry will be withdrawn from its use at Camp Lancaster and replaced by other tents and means of transportation to be sent from Fort Davis and will be returned without delay to this place, or the posts from which they were drawn."[46]

Captain Carpenter was from Maine, and graduated thirty-fifth in the West Point Class of 1840. At the beginning of the Civil War he would be promoted to major and assigned to the Nineteenth Infantry. Brevetted to lieutenant colonel for gallant and meritorious service at Shiloh, he was killed during the battle of Murfreesboro, Tennessee, in December 1862. Ordered to Camp Lancaster with Carpenter were 2nd Lts. Samuel Reynolds and George Williams. Reynolds, who served less than three months at the Post, graduated from West Point, and would resign his commission in 1861 to join the Confederate Army in his native Virginia. A West Point graduate from New York, Williams would serve fourteen months at Camp Lancaster. He was active in the Western Theater during the Civil War, with distinguished service at Corinth and Vicksburg, Mississippi. He retired in 1870 with the rank of major and died April 2, 1889.[47]

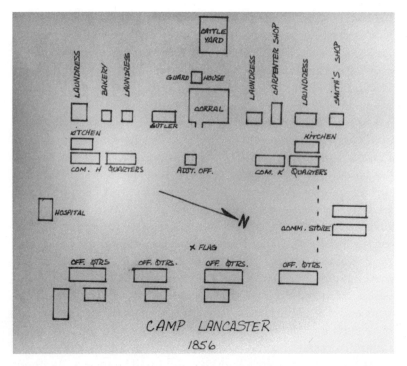

Camp Lancaster, 1856. Redrawn by Jerry Harlan from Col. Joseph Mansfield's *Inspection Report of Fort Lancaster, June 10–11, 1856. Courtesy Jerry Harlan.*

Companies H and K settled in to make a home of their new post. With their primary mission to patrol the Lower Road between Fort Clark and Fort Davis, their mere presence also served as a local deterrent. With good water, fuel and shelter, this area of the Pecos River and Live Oak Creek was the junction of several Indian trails. A permanent army post denied the use of the region as an Indian camp. Within four months, in December 1856, acting department commander, Col. Albert Sidney Johnston reported that Fort Davis and Fort Lancaster were, "indispensable for keeping open the communication from New Mexico."[48]

As winter approached, the first concern was shelter for the troops. The first structures were temporary in nature, and were built with the materials at hand by the soldiers who received extra-duty pay. These quarters were uncomfortable and provided little protection from the elements. The most common form of construction were *jacales*, a basic structure of vertical pickets or planks set in the ground with thatch or canvas for roofing. The bakery, carpenter shop, hospital, and several other buildings were of this type. The officers' quarters, of which there were four, were constructed of adobe and probably thatched. Being important to the survival of the garrison, the quartermaster and commissary stores were structures with stone walls and canvas roofs.

Several of the original structures at the post were an early attempt at prefabrication. Named for the officer who developed them, Lt. Parmenas Taylor Turnley, they were Turnley Portable Buildings. Available in two sizes, the Turnley buildings were inexpensive, could be reused, and were transportable by wagon. Designed for use as a barracks, hospital, or storeroom, the larger size was eighteen by forty feet. The smaller version, fifteen by thirty feet, came with a moveable partition and was designed as quarters for two officers. Boards ten inches wide by eight feet long were divided by stanchions and set vertically into a top and bottom plate with corner posts. Doors and windows came as complete sets, and iron bolts joined the structure. The larger units weighed approximately three thousand pounds, and the smaller ones approximately two thousand. Transported completely disassembled in army wagons, one took three men three hours to erect. An additional hour was required for roofing, which consisted of panels covered with asphalt paper attached with battens. Turnley, a first lieutenant in the First Infantry, was assigned to K Company. However, he was on detached duty until October 1856. At that time he was promoted to captain and transferred, and never actually served at Fort Lancaster.[49]

With the construction of shelter the garrison settled into the routine of frontier military life. Since no medical officer was initially available, Captain Carpenter contracted with a civilian, J. D. B. Stillman, to provide medical service. Dr. Stillman was an interesting and unique choice. He was, in addition to being a trained physician, a well-traveled adventurer and an excellent observer. Concurrent with his medical appointment at Camp Lancaster was his assignment as a journalist for the New York City *Crayon*. Reporting on his western adventures, Stillman wrote two letters from Camp Lancaster, one in October, and one in November 1855. The *Crayon* published them in February and March 1856. Both provide a remarkable view of the post soon after it was established.

In his October 1855 letter, published in February of the next year, Stillman writes, "to check the incursions of Indians, the War Department establishes posts at the most important watering-places. The one at which I now write is near the junction of the 'live Oak Creek' with the Pecos, about eighty miles from where the latter empties into the Rio Grande. The creek is seven miles long, and affords a constant supply of clear, good water: on it are several groves of small live oaks; there are also a few gum-trees, and hackberries, willows, grape-vines, and rank weeds almost conceal the water, while they mark the course of the creek through a wide, deep valley." As a close observer of his surroundings, Stillman provides a substantial inventory of the abundant plant and animal life in the area, including black bear, wolf, and fox. Hunting was a regular pastime with quail, turkey, duck, deer, and antelope being common game. However, he writes that, "there is one drawback to hunting in this part of Texas . . . [for] one never knows when he leaves camp to go any distance, but he may be made game of himself before he returns."[50]

Even as a temporary member of the garrison, Stillman was familiar with the shortcomings of both the mission and the methods of soldiering in this desolate country. He writes, "what can they do without horses against these Arabs of the American desert? As well might dragoons be used as marines on the deck of a frigate." He was impressed with the officers he met, but critical of the War Department and the methods the War Department and army staff imposed upon the troops in the field. He notes that the troops should move away from the road in order to, "hunt the Indian in his own style; to endure long marches without cooking, without baggage in silence; to hover about the track of the savage where ever it leads; to be a shadow to a shadow."[51]

Living with the officers of the post, Stillman found them to be

A Turnley Portable Building. By Beth Francell. *Courtesy Beth Francell.*

worthy companions working at an impossible task. "I have every reason to be proud as an American of the character of our army officers; one never meets with a discourtesy from the graduates of West Point, or sees one that is not every inch a soldier, and it seems entirely out of place to send such men to hunt Indians. It seems like a sad waste of science and talent." Stillman developed a great "sympathy for the young officer who enters the service full of ambition for advancement and distinction, and finds himself an exile, banished . . . to some frontier post, away from the elevating influences of home. Long marches, much danger, no honor, and great privations, and if by favor of his superior he is permitted to return to the haunts of civilized men, the savings of years are spent to defray the expenses of the journey."[52]

While at Lancaster, Stillman became close friends with Captain Carpenter, and much admired his two hunting dogs, Cola and

Quail. He credited the dogs with being more effective sentries at night than the guards on post. "The readiness with which the dogs bark at night, on the approach of any unusual object, contributes more to the safety of individuals going about after dark than anything else. It is not an uncommon casualty to have a man shot through the body with an arrow in the dark, and even in the daytime, and yet no Indian be seen. Such was the fate of a musician of one of the companies now here, while it was encamped on Devil's River." The Devil's River incident refers to the march from Fort Duncan to establish the post.[53]

His friendship with Carpenter, and the lack of company officers gave Stillman the opportunity for adventures not normally part of the role of the post surgeon. "The command here is very busily engaged in preparing winter quarters, and as the Captain had expressed a desire to send out a party to explore a shorter route to Howard Springs, but could not spare an officer to go with it, I proposed to undertake it." Howard Springs, or Well on some maps, was the nearest source of water east along the road from the post. Mounted on mules and accompanied by three of the best hunters, Pvts. Richard Young and James Beardall, and Musician Thomas Dennen, Stillman took command of his patrol. Finding no route passable for wagons, the party was nonetheless successful in the hunt, bringing fresh venison into camp.[54]

A few days later Stillman was asked to accompany Carpenter to the head of Live Oak Creek, where the captain hoped to find a grove of trees with one large enough to supply a flagpole. This time he did not make the trip, having "mounted in haste, I touched the mule with my spurs, when there ensued a series of evolutions not laid down in cavalry tactics, and entirely unbecoming the high position which for a moment I held. One movement, more vigorous than the rest, projected me, rifle, spurs and all, according to the law of projectiles, into which my West Point friends had not duly indoctrinated me, over his ears, and I suspect over my own; but upon that point I had no positive impression, nor as to the point of contact with the ground." Unhurt Stillman concluded, "as to the mule, I judged his conduct to be perfectly justifiable, according to the laws of honor of the land. He did no more up to that moment than he was compelled to do, to maintain self-respect. It was not necessary that he should continue to kick at me after I was down; but then his ears were so long that he could not help it. I concluded to permit the commander to get his own flagstaff, and repaired to my tent to write."[55]

On October 12, Captain Carpenter determined to explore the head of Live Oak Creek. Stillman, Private Beardall and Musician Dennen accompanied him, as did Pvt. Patrick McCulloch and a civilian teamster who were driving a wagon and team to bring back poles to the post. Stillman describes Carpenter as a dashing figure who, "rode his favorite blood horse, 'Driver,' and was accompanied by his two dogs. His 'six-shooter' hung at the horn of his saddle, and across the saddle in front of him he carried his shotgun. Over one shoulder hung his powder-flask, and at the other his shot belt; an ivory whistle, fashioned after a dog's head, was suspended at a button hole of his hunting jacket."[56]

Arriving without incident at the head of Live Oak Creek, the soldiers were left to cut poles while Carpenter and Stillman proceeded towards a smaller grove. Expecting to find wild turkeys they instead encountered a band of Indians, "well mounted, armed with shields, bows and arrows, lances, and a few with guns; they were painted and bedevilled for war." Retreating to their working party, haste was made in loading the wagon for a return to the post. Separated from his companions when the attack occurred, Stillman saw the teamster overwhelmed, and was himself pursued as he turned towards the fort. Upon his return, "I reported the whole party killed, as I had no doubt they were, before I 'broke' for camp. The probable death of Captain Carpenter, who was so much beloved by the whole command, created a most painful situation. There was a hurrying of men to arms, and a party started off on foot at quick time."[57]

At dusk the captain, wounded in the hand, returned to the post with the other men. Private McCulloch had been struck in the foot by an arrow. Beardall and Dennen were uninjured. While Carpenter's wound was dressed, he explained what happened to the rest of the party after Stillman's separation. As the teamster abandoned the wagon and was overwhelmed, the other four dismounted and prepared for an attack. Moving cautiously in the direction of the fort, they were confronted first by a mounted attack at a distance, and then by an attack on foot with the Indians using the scrub for cover. Carpenter had his men hold their fire until the Indians were within fifty yards, at which time they were able to return an effective fire. In describing the melee Stillman writes, "Dennen and Beardall were musicians to Company K, and from boyhood had served in the army on the frontiers, were expert hunters, and cool as if it were only deer that they had to shoot. Beardall felt the brush of an arrow and saw the Indian who had shot it, and disregarding all others, he held his rifle to the spot where he saw him disappear behind a bush, until he rose again, when he fired, and the savage fell without sending his arrow."[58]

Meanwhile the two Indian leaders singled out Carpenter. Protected by shields and armed with bows and lances, they attacked from two directions. "The Captain held his horse and shot-gun by the left hand, and in his right his six-shooter, pointing the latter at the chiefs alternately. He had already fired three shots, and his antagonists had advanced to twelve paces from him." One arrow struck his horse, one severed the shoulder strap holding his shot bag, one lodged in his boot without piercing his leg, one penetrated his heavy coat, and a fifth struck his hand.[59]

"It was a critical moment for him," continued Stillman. "He had abandoned all hope of saving his own life, and became intent only on selling it dearly. If his next shot failed he was lost; he levelled his pistol upon the fierce chief in front of him, who stopped, the more perfectly to protect his body with his shield, when by a quick movement of the pistol, he brought it to cover the other chief, who was closing upon him with his spear, and struck him full in the chest before he could raise his shield." Turning quickly to counter his other adversary Carpenter found, "that a cartridge from Dennen's gun had laid him low, just at the moment that he was about to spring on the Captain." At this point the attack ended. The Indians disappeared, and within an hour the rescue party from the fort arrived.[60]

The Indians were identified as Apaches, and by following their trail it could be determined that they had carefully planned their

A Schott del.   Lith. of Sarony & Co. New York.

LIPAN—WARRIOR.

An Apache warrior. From Maj. William Emory, *Report on the United States and Mexican Boundary Survey* (Washington, 1857; reprint, Texas State Historical Association, 1987). The primary adversaries of the soldiers at Fort Lancaster were the Apache Indians. Arthur Schott, an artist on Emory's survey, captured this image of a Lipan Apache, one of the tribes consistently harassing travelers along the Lower Road. *Photograph courtesy Center for American History, University of Texas at Austin. CN 09465.*

ambush. Stillman notes that "their dispositions were well made, and the whole plan of attack showed great sagacity, and would have been successful in cutting off every man in the party, were it not that they wanted victory too cheap." Two days later a supply train between Lancaster and Fort Davis had all of their animals stolen, but it was not determined if this was the same party. Soon after, Stillman prepared to depart Camp Lancaster on the rest of his adventure west. "In a few days I shall again be upon the road to leave a dreary country and a pleasant camp, where I have experienced many kindnesses and cordial greetings."[61]

In January 1856, Asst. Surgeon George Taylor replaced Stillman. On February 2, 1856, Captain Carpenter turned over the command of the post to Capt. Robert S. Granger, and took four months leave. Granger, who would become the permanent commanding officer, arrived with enough reinforcements to bring both garrison companies to seventy-nine men apiece. A native of Ohio, Granger graduated twenty-eighth in the West Point Class of 1838. Assigned to the First Infantry, he was promoted captain in 1847. At the beginning of the Civil War, he was appointed brigadier general of volunteers and served with distinction throughout the conflict. Reverting to lieutenant colonel at the end of the war, he served in the infantry until he retired in 1873. He died on April 25, 1894.[62]

In June 1856, Camp Lancaster received its first official inspection. Inspector General, Col. Joseph K. F. Mansfield, in the process of inspecting the forts in Texas, arrived on June 9. He spent three days on Live Oak Creek. The manner in which Mansfield reports conditions does not hide the fact that life there was rather bleak and uneventful. The inspector general found a garrison of 150 men, a surgeon, and three officers. However, only ninety-six men were available for duty, and there should have been six officers. Three officers were on detached duty. Fifty-four men were either confined to the guardhouse, in hospital, or on extra or detached duty.[63]

Mansfield inspected the companies and found that "Company H. was in full uniform and in excellent order—quarters in a Turnley portable building and a hackale (*jacal*) and canvas mess hall and kitchen—no iron bedsteads—police good—2 laundresses—3 desertions in 1855 & 3 in 1856—books in good order—Company property & ordnance in a hackale in good order." Company K was also in good order, with three laundresses. There were four desertions in 1855, and none in 1856. He found much of the company equipment in poor condition, and "condemned to be broken up 15 muskets & 1 rifle & 1 Colts pistols & to be dropped 20 cartridge boxes, 22 cap pouches, 4 cartridge box belts, 9 bayonette scabbards, 45 cartridge box belt plates, 3 cartridge box plates, 21 rifle slings, 7 waist belt plates." Ammunition was in short supply. However, on June 7 the Ordnance Department in San Antonio ordered ten thousand musket cartridges to be delivered to the post.[64]

Mansfield found that fatigue duty, escorts for travelers on the road, and patrols of detachments of less than company strength made up the garrison routine. Half of the command consisted of recruits, and "they could not drill as skirmishers. Nor could they drill at the bayonet. I dispensed with Target firing for the same reason. All of the officers at this post were active industrious and willing but the labor of instructing inferior recruits, by the Captain of a Company at the squad drill is great and most of it should fall on subalterns. The non-commissioned officers, in most instances, are not properly qualified. Add to this the labour of building a post in such a locality."[65]

The military qualities of the garrison were not the only things that the inspector general found lacking. The hospital was a temporary *jacal* with a dispensary and quarters for the steward, but there was no ward. The guardhouse was also a *jacal*. Since the post was established, there had been seventy-six men confined, six for drunkenness by liquor obtained from travelers on the road. The post sutler, a man named Lepier (Savier in Stillman's letters), was allowed to sell liquor only by permit. Mansfield commented, "I presume the great error is in enlisting confirmed drunkards who desire nothing better than to get drunk & Lay in the guard house."[66]

Lt. George Williams, H Company, was acting quartermaster and commissary officer. In his charge was a stone storehouse with a canvas roof, a carpenter shop, a blacksmith shop, and a corral. His quartermaster staff consisted of a sergeant, three teamsters, a carpenter, and a herder. There is no mention of a blacksmith. The commissary was a stone building with a staff consisting of one sergeant. Williams was also responsible for the bakery, only a *jacal* with a canvas roof, but it had a good oven and good bread. To add to his duties Williams was also the recruiting officer, a task that required him to encourage re-enlistment from the garrison.

To house the three line officers and the surgeon, there were four temporary adobe buildings. The post possessed a good parade ground, a flagstaff, and two small gardens. Due to the dry climate the inspector general was doubtful about the success of growing vegetables. He reported only one rain since May 11 and the temperature was over one hundred degrees. Concluding his report Mansfield found the two-company garrison adequate but he recommended that one should be mounted on mules and both should have a full compliment of officers. He requested that rifled muskets be supplied to the garrison, "for the Indians when running must be reached at a long range . . . or not at all."[67]

Mansfield described the Indians inhabiting the country near Lancaster as Apaches. They were prone to strike the Lower Road when least expected, and were always difficult to find. On his return from Lancaster to San Antonio via Fort Clark, he and his men had to render aid to a party of drovers with a herd of cattle headed for New Mexico. One man had been killed and one wounded. Mansfield detached five of his escort to accompany the herd safely to Camp Lancaster.[68]

While the inspector general found that Camp Lancaster "with some assistance from the quartermaster [Department] can be made comfortable," a visitor two months later in August had another opinion. Lydia Spencer Lane was the wife of an officer in the Regiment of Mounted Rifles, which had been ordered to New Mexico. She accompanied her husband on the march, and they paused at Camp Lancaster on August 2. In her journal she writes, "there were several Army posts along our route, and to arrive at one was a pleasant variety in the irksomeness of the long days. Camp Lancaster was the first we passed—and was the worst station I had seen in Texas, but the ladies I met at the post seemed cheerful and contented. We dined with Captain and Mrs. R. S.

Granger."[69]

As the first year of its existence came to a close, changes were in store for the post. While many of the structures were still temporary in nature and the garrison was still ill-adapted to its mission, the camp was to be upgraded to Fort Lancaster.

4.
Fort Lancaster

ON AUGUST 12, 1856, A YEAR AND A DAY after it was founded, orders were issued to upgrade the post to Fort Lancaster. Due to slow communications, this order was not received on Live Oak Creek until September 25. Issued from headquarters in San Antonio, Order Number 53 read: "The post known as 'Camp Lancaster' on the El Paso Road at the crossing of Live Oak Creek, will be considered on the same footing with regard to permanency as the other frontier posts in the Department, and will in future be called Fort Lancaster." Henceforth a serious effort would be made to upgrade and make permanent the various structures that made up the post.[70]

In December, Lieutenant Williams transferred, leaving Granger and Carpenter as the only line officers in residence. In January 1857, Asst. Surgeon George Taylor led a detachment in pursuit of Apaches. While this was not one of the normal duties of the post doctor, it was understandable with the lack of company officers. In February two new officers were posted to Fort Lancaster. Second Lt. Alexander M. Haskell arrived during the month, and immediately replaced Taylor in the field. Haskell was commissioned a second lieutenant in the First Infantry in June 1856. Fort Lancaster appears to be his first duty station. He resigned his commission at the beginning of the Civil War and served with the Sixth Texas Volunteers.[71]

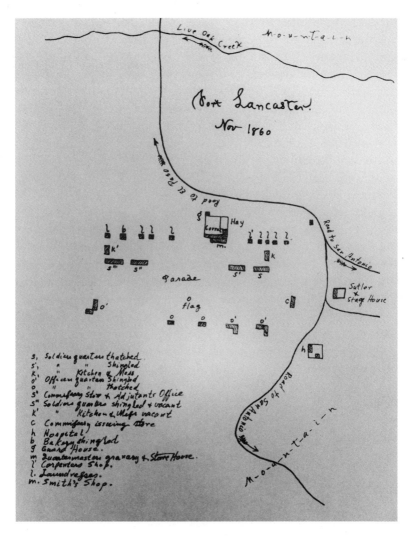

Fort Lancaster, 1860. From Col. Joseph Mansfield's *Inspection of Fort Lancaster, November 20, 1860. Photograph courtesy author's collection.*

The second new officer was John Pitts Sherburne from New Hampshire. He received an appointment to West Point, but was dismissed for a deficiency in chemistry. However, his brother-in-law was 1st Lt. Amiel Weeks Whipple, the commanding officer for the transcontinental railroad survey of the Thirty-fifth Parallel. Sherburne received an appointment as an assistant meteorologist and surveyor. Once the expedition reached California, he remained there for the next two years. Sherburne married in 1855, and with a new child and few prospects he joined the army in June 1857. Commissioned a second lieutenant, he was assigned to Fort Lancaster. While stationed at Fort Lancaster, another child was born. During the Civil War, Sherburne rose to colonel-in-chief of cavalry for the Department of the Gulf. He mustered out in 1870, went back to California, and became an inspector at the U.S. Customs House in San Francisco. He died January 9, 1880.[72]

Lieutenant Sherburne was appointed quartermaster, reporting to chief quartermaster of the Department of Texas, Maj. D. H. Vinton. On May 27, 1857, he wrote his superior a letter that provides a description of Fort Lancaster and the progress that was being made to create a permanent post. Less than a year before, Inspector General Mansfield found only four temporary quarters for officers. Now there were five, "built of stone and adobies . . . thatched with grass cut by fatigue men." Captain Granger had a Turnley building attached to his quarters, and Captain Carpenter had half of one attached to his. The garrison was still housed in Turnley buildings, but barracks of stone and adobe were under construction.[73]

The kitchens and mess halls for the companies were of stone with thatch. However, the bakeries, blacksmith's shop, forage storeroom, harness house, and four quarters for laundresses were *jacals*. All were due for replacement. Construction of permanent structures was slowed by the lack of wood available for lumber. Sherburne reports that "lime stone to be had in abundance, roofing very scarce, none to be had nearer than the Devils River, not more than 200 feet of Lumber now at the post, and scarcely any material for Building purposes to be had without considerable trouble and difficulty, adobies can be made at the Post by fatigue parties. Lime can be procured at the Post by burning it, but consumes a great deal of wood."[74]

Wood for all purposes was scarce. Lumber was hauled from San Antonio, or from Fort Davis, which operated a sawmill. "I beg also to inform you that the commanding officer here will send a party to Fort Davis early next week and will avail himself of the means mentioned in your letter of the 14th Inst. with regard to procuring lumber at Fort Davis," wrote Sherburne. Wood for heat and to fuel the bakery was obtained along Live Oak Creek and the Pecos, but was as far as six miles away and required intense labor by fatigue parties.[75]

Commissary and quartermaster supplies were shipped along the Lower Road from San Antonio. They were received from private contractors to the army at a cost "so far known from Ft. Clark to this post at $2.621/4 per 100 lbs., transportation between Ft. Clark and San Antonio not known." Hay for forage could be cut along the Pecos in the fall, but it was of poor quality. Good quality beef on the hoof was obtained by government contract at thirteen cents per pound.[76]

Sherburne was asked to assess the condition of the Lower Road, provide the distances from one fort to another, and name the streams and the conditions of their crossings. To this query he stated that the road was generally "rough and hilly." The distance to Fort Clark was 174 miles and Fort Davis was 158 miles. There were numerous stream and river crossings between these posts and Fort Lancaster, but none were bridged. From his letter it appears that the road was well trafficked.[77]

July 1857 was to be the most active month in the existence of Fort Lancaster. On July 9, Lt. Edward Beale and his expedition of camels arrived at the post on the way west to New Mexico. Breaking their previous camp at 3:00 A.M., Beale reported that "we travelled fifteen miles and encamped two miles from Fort Lancaster, on Live Oak Creek. While at breakfast, some of the officers called and invited us to the post, of which kindness we shall avail ourselves." Of the camels Beale wrote, "we are busy today repairing their saddles and doctoring their wounded backs, and to effect this purpose I shall go no further, but remain here until tomorrow." Describing the area, Beale wrote, "Live Oak Creek is a clear and beautiful stream of cool and sweet water; the grass very fine, and wood (oak, mesquite, and willow), abundant. Just before descending into the valley of the stream we came to a very steep,

Camels Crossing a River. By Henry S. Sindall. Watercolor and gauche on paper, ca. 1860. One of the experimental army camel expeditions through West Texas. *Photograph courtesy Amon Carter Museum, Fort Worth, Texas. Acc. No. 1973.1.*

rocky hill, overlooking a valley of great beauty and graceful shape. The sides of the hills were covered with the most brilliant verdure and flowers, and our long train, as it wound down the steep descent, and became stretched out on the winding road through the valley, presented a scene of uncommon beauty."[78]

Accompanying the camel expedition was May Humphreys Stacey, a seventeen-year-old boy out for adventure. In his journal he reports the tragedy that marred the visit to Fort Lancaster. "This afternoon a very melancholy fact was communicated to us. Captain Lee, the officer second in command at Fort Davis, who had travelled with us from Fort Clark where we met him, had the misfortune to lose his son fifteen months old." Capt. Arthur T. Lee was returning from leave with his family, and had proceeded directly to Fort Lancaster. Lee was an accomplished artist, documenting his travels through Texas during this period. However, events at Fort Lancaster were such that he made no visual record of this visit.[79]

The funeral was held that afternoon, and Stacey recorded, "we rigged ourselves out in the best clothes we had, got underway from camp about ten and drove up to the post and alighted. We were introduced to the officers who appeared to be very clever young men. They are pretty gay and as usual drink their grog without winking." At this isolated garrison even a funeral became a social event, and the camels became the center of attention. "Captain Carpenter, after being invited by Mr. Beale, mounted and took a short ride. He expressed himself with much delight at the gait and said that after one became used to the motion he would prefer the camel to a mule."[80]

After the service, Carpenter and his wife invited the visitors for a meal, and Stacey described the affair. "We availed ourselves of the invitation with an alacrity that was very amusing even to ourselves. The dinner consisted of ham and eggs, elegant rolls and butter, and claret, and I can say that I never tasted better in my life. The dessert took down anything of the kind that I have ever tasted. Peaches preserved, with cream, and fruit cake. To us who have been living on salt junk and hard biscuit it was a treat that we will always remember with lively feelings of pleasure." After this dinner prepared by Mrs. Carpenter, "one of the cleverest little women we have seen in Texas," the camel expedition left for Fort Davis.[81]

In late July 1857, the most significant action in the history of the post occurred. On the evening of July 24, the monthly express from San Antonio was attacked twenty-five miles west of Fort Lancaster by a band of sixty Mescalero Apaches. The express consisted of an ambulance and wagon escorted by Sgt. Ernest Schroeder with six men of the Eighth Infantry from Fort Davis. They were accompanied by a wood detail of six men from Fort Lancaster under the command of Sergeant Libby. As the Indians approached, the two sergeants ordered the teams unhitched and the men to take shelter behind the wagons. As one group of Indians held up a white flag and exchanged shouts in Spanish, another group crept up a nearby ravine. As Schroeder sought protection behind a wagon, he shouted, according to Sergeant Libby's later report, "look out Sergt for the sons of bitches they will get the advantage of you if they can &

don't put yourself in danger." At that instant a bullet through the heart killed Schroeder. Sergeant Libby took command and ordered a retreat to Fort Lancaster. Firing as they withdrew, the men were ordered by Libby to abandon the body of Sergeant Schroeder after carrying it for over a mile. With the onset of night the Indians gave up the pursuit, and the escort returned to Fort Lancaster about three o'clock the next morning. Five Indians were reported killed, and the official inquiry concluded that "the conduct of the sergeants commanding the mail escort and the wood party is represented as perfectly correct, and it seems to have been gallant and judicious."[82]

Upon reaching the fort, Captain Granger organized a pursuit under Lieutenant Haskell. Camped at the post was a detachment of forty-six men from Fort Davis under the command of Lt. Edward Hartz and Lt. Edward Read. Hartz asked to join Haskell, and by seniority took command of both units. Eighty men were loaded into wagons, and the canvas covers were drawn. Disguised as a provision train, this force started for Fort Davis. Taking the bait, a group of thirty to forty Indians attacked forty-five miles west of Fort Lancaster. As the Apaches realized it was an ambush, the infantry opened fire.

The Indians then withdrew, and Hartz deployed half his men as skirmishers, ordering them to advance. Hoping to burn out the wagons and create a smoke screen for another attack, the Apaches set fire to the prairie. Hartz recalled his men and moved the wagons to a bare depression, over which the flames passed. The skirmishers advanced once more, and at that point the Apaches gave up the fight. Hartz and his command continued west until they met the eastbound mail at Comanche Springs, which they escorted back to Fort Lancaster. To the garrison at Fort Lancaster this was a major action. In his report on this action, Lieutenant Hartz was critical of the lack of mounted troops. Without horses or mules he was unable to pursue the retreating Apaches. As he wrote in his report, "the impunity with which attacks have been made in the past week and the powerlessness of infantry to act with advantage against the bands infesting the road . . . show conclusively that the Indians are in virtual possession of the road." While no soldiers and only two Indians were reported killed, this type of skirmish was more prevalent than fully supported and coordinated campaigns.[83]

In August 1857, a year after the post was made permanent, five thousand dollars was allocated for the "erection and repairs of public buildings at Fort Lancaster." That month the garrison was also short on basic supplies. The War Department commanding officer, Gen. David Twiggs, approved "taking 7 barrels of salt pork from the train to Fort Davis," and noted that "the supplies for Fort Lancaster have departed San Antonio." In September the routine of the post was pleasantly broken by the arrival of eighteen members of the First Infantry Band. They stayed at the fort for two months.[84]

During September there was an attempt to solve the problem of pursuing Indians with infantry. Within the army the value of mounting infantry on horses had been debated for some time. In August the War Department ordered General Twiggs to authorize the mounting of twenty men at the following forts: Davis, Lancaster, Chadbourne, and Duncan. The orders stated that the men "will be selected for their horsemanship and efficiency as mounted men," and "they will be held accountable for the care of their animals." These soldiers "will be armed with carbines and revolvers. Until carbines can be provided, muskets will be used instead." On September 21, orders from the the Department's assistant adjutant general, Bvt. Capt. John Withers were sent to Captain Granger. "The General Commanding the Department directs me to say, that you will send to this city, as soon as possible a subaltern and at least six enlisted men from your command to take up, from here to Fort Lancaster, the horses intended for the mounting of a portion of the infantry at the latter post." Little opinion about the effectiveness of this endeavor is noted in the monthly *Post Returns* or the correspondence files.[85]

In November, Captain Granger was ordered to lead a scouting party to find a shortcut to Comanche Springs. He was also to determine if there was a suitable location along this route for a new Fort Lancaster. During this same period, Lieutenant Haskell explored the vicinity of Comanche Springs. The distance between

Fort Lancaster and Fort Davis was too great for effective patrols, and the water source at Comanche Springs provided a haven for the Indians attacking the Lower Road. However, the army was not yet willing to commit to the costs of constructing a new fort.[86]

A general court-martial was ordered convened at Fort Lancaster in October. The purpose was the "trial of Private John McGowen of Company H, 1st Infy., and any other prisoners as may be brought before it." All four company officers, Granger, Carpenter, Haskell, and Sherburne were assigned to the court, as was 1st Lt. Theodore Fink of the Eighth Infantry. Lieutenant Fink was most likely stationed at Fort Davis. Asst. Surgeon George Taylor was assigned the role of judge advocate. This Court convened on November 16 with Captain Granger as president. He reported the findings on December 14. The sentences of the two soldiers who were tried, 1st Sgt. Thomas Wilson and Private McGowen, illustrate the nature of the discipline problems in the frontier army.[87]

Sergeant Wilson was charged twice with conduct prejudicial to good order and military discipline. The first charge was the failure to obey an order from Lieutenant Sherburne to turn over rations to Pvt. George Butler. Sherburne stated that Wilson, "did refuse to obey said order, and did reply 'I recognize no such authority,' or words to that effect: This at Fort Lancaster, Texas, on, or about, the 13th day of May, 1857." The second charge related to Wilson's role as commissary clerk where he did, "issue, or allow to be issued, dispose of, or allow to be disposed of, in an improper manner, without authority, and without accounting for, forty-one pounds of crushed sugar, more or less, in charge of the Acting Assistant Commissary of Subsistence."[88]

Private McGowen faced the same charge, in his case for being "so much under the influence of spirituous liquor as to be unable to properly perform the duties of a soldier." A further charge stated that "when ordered By Corporal Adolph Single, of Company H, 1st Infantry, the Corporal of the Guard, to put out a cigar, which the said McGowen was smoking in the Quarter-Master's yard, (there being a standing order against smoking in that place), did refuse to obey said order, and did reply, 'you can put me in the guardhouse if you wish to, I want to go there,' or words to that effect."[89]

Wilson was found guilty of the first charge, and not guilty of the second. McGowen was found guilty of both of the charges levied against him. For his transgressions, Wilson was reduced in rank to private and forfeited three months pay. McGowen was sentenced to forfeit five dollars of his monthly pay for three months, and to be confined to hard labor for the same period of time.[90]

In February 1858, both Captain Granger and Captain Carpenter were in San Antonio for court-martial duty, and Lieutenant Haskell was in command of the fort. He and Sherburne were the only officers present. This would be the only month in the history of the post that neither Granger nor Carpenter was in command. During this same month enough replacements arrived to bring the garrison to 152 men present. Both companies now averaged seventy men, twenty more than previously. During March, 1st Lt. Walter Jones, assigned to H Company arrived, and would remain with the garrison for one year until transferred to Camp Stockton. A native of the District of Columbia, Jones would resign from federal service, and join the Confederate Army where he served for the duration of the conflict.[91]

In April 1858, Captain Granger took six months leave, and then was placed on recruiting duty for three months. Captain Carpenter was once again in command. A civilian guide was hired in May, and paid forty-five dollars per month. He remained in service until February 1859. Often at individual posts, civilians familiar with the area were hired to lead patrols and scout for Indians.

During the summer and fall of 1858 there was no notable activity listed in the *Post Returns* other than the day-to-day routine. In January 1859, Joseph R. Smith replaced George Taylor as surgeon. Smith joined the Medical Corps in 1854, served in the Federal Army during the Civil War, and retired as colonel surgeon in 1895. First Lt. James B. Greene also joined the garrison. Little is known of Greene, except that he was from New York, graduated from West Point in 1851, and died in June 1861.[92]

In early 1859, there was a move to establish a new fort between Fort Lancaster and Fort Davis. The distance between these two points was too far for effective defense of the Lower Road. In January, Lieutenant Sherburne was leading a scouting party at

Escondido Springs. By February his patrol was at Comanche Springs. During March, Lieutenant Haskell was also at Comanche Springs. As the senior officer present, he must be given credit for the establishment of the new post, Camp Stockton, later upgraded to Fort Stockton.[93]

In his April *Post Return*, Captain Granger wrote that "Co. 'H' 1st Infty. left to take post at Camp Stockton Texas on the 12th day of April/59, per Spl. Ord. No. 20, dated San Antonio March 23, 1859." In the absence of Captain Carpenter and Lieutenant Jones, Lieutenant Sherburne marched the eighty men of H Company to Camp Stockton. Since Lieutenant Haskell was assigned to K Company, he returned to Fort Lancaster to rejoin Captain Granger, Lieutenant Greene, and the eighty men of the company. From April 1859, until the post was abandoned, K Company would remain the only unit of the garrison.[94]

The loss of H Company produced only small changes. The demand for supplies was reduced, and there was more available room. The commissary officer utilized half of one of the vacant barracks as a storeroom, and the other half was used as an office for the adjutant. By this time most of the structures at the fort were of stone and adobe, and the loss of one company did not add much to the burden of fatigue duty. Escort duty along the road had always been carried out by small detachments, and with the establishment of the new post at Comanche Springs the distance to protect was decreased.

In April, a week after the departure of H Company, Fort Lancaster became the starting point for a major patrol by I Company of the Second Cavalry under the command of Capt. Albert Brackett. With fifteen days' meat ration from the stores at Fort Lancaster, Brackett marched his men along the Comanche War Trail. Passing Comanche Springs with its newly arrived garrison, the patrol turned south towards the Rio Grande. Brackett and his command reached the abandoned Spanish presidio of San Vicente on April 30. When his scout found a large band of Indians ten miles below his camp, Brackett attacked. In the melee two Indians were killed and one wounded. No soldiers were injured and Brackett commended three men for their courage.[95]

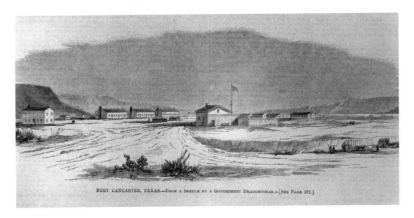

Fort Lancaster, Texas. From a Sketch by a Government Draftsman, *Harper's Weekly*, March 23, 1861. This is the only know illustration of Fort Lancaster, and was published days after the post was abandoned. *Photograph courtesy author's collection.*

By now the command was out of rations and far from home. Presidio, on the far side of the Big Bend, was the closest town. Without the means to cross some of the most desolate country in Texas, Brackett decided to cross the Rio Grande into Mexico. The patrol arrived at the village of San Carlos on May 5, and Brackett was able to resupply. Lacking the means to return to Fort Lancaster, the command marched to Presidio and then to Fort Davis, where it arrived on May 15. Brackett and his men performed one of the most remarkable scouting expeditions of the period.[96]

In July, Pvt. Henry Metz of the Eighth Infantry "delivered himself up as a deserter." The next month Captain Granger had command of the fort alone while Lieutenants Haskell and Greene went to Fort Davis for court-martial duty. In September, Lieutenant Haskell was reported under arrest, but no cause was given and no action was taken. In November, Musician George Kelly of the First Dragoons was apprehended as a deserter, and was waiting for transportation back to his company for punishment. Little, other than discipline problems, seemed worth reporting in the monthly *Post Returns.*[97]

The year 1860 was, according to the record provided by the *Post Returns* and correspondence files, the most uneventful in the fort's history. Lieutenant Haskell, possibly as a result of his earlier arrest, was on leave and detached duty for the year, while Captain Granger, Lieutenant Greene, and Asst. Surgeon Taylor served as the garrison officers. However, in late November, Inspector General Joseph Mansfield arrived for another inspection.

Arriving on November 20, the inspector general found a much different post than the one he had visited four years earlier. "It was inspected by me in 1856. There were then two companies here, & the quarters, and accommodations quite inferior. The soldiers then occupied the Turnley Cottages for quarters. Since that time they have proved a failure as I then anticipated, and their place has been filled by good adobe buildings, with wooden floors, & about half of them shingled and the remainder with thatched roofs, and all the command comfortably lodged."[98]

The garrison consisted of four sergeants, three corporals, two musicians, and fifty-seven privates. One sergeant and seven men were on escort duty, and one man was absent at the insane asylum in Washington. Discounting those absent as well as the cooks, baker, teamsters, guards, and prisoners, there were forty men on parade. "These men were on inspection in uniform, except that some had dark, & some light blue pantaloons; and were well equipped for the field, in excellent order in every respect. They passed in review in quick & double quick time well, and as skirmishers; & thro' the manual of the bayonet exercise well." Mansfield reported that the garrison performed the best target practice he witnessed on his inspection tour.[99]

Since 1857 twelve men had deserted, and the inspector general commented that "the few desertions are in my opinion, in some degree, an index of good and judicious discipline." The post guardhouse held four prisoners, and was a stone and thatch building attached to the corral. The weapons were kept next to the first sergeant's room, and "the arms, camp and garrison equippage are well cared for. There were 76 rifled muskets, 2 Harpers Ferry rifles, 2 Colts pistols, 2500 blank cartridges, 7400 musket ball cartridges, 700 Colts pistol ball cartridges, 74 canteens, 60 knapsacks, 71 haversacks." There were four laundresses, each with separate quarters.[100]

The post staff consisted of ordnance sergeant Edward Brenner, Surgeon Smith, and hospital steward William Webster. The condition of the hospital was one of the few problems that Mansfield encountered, but one for which he found the solution. "The hospital is a very poor adobe building, braced up on one end. But as this post was originally built for two companies, there is a set of soldiers quarters that could readily be used as a hospital now vacant. There is one cook, one nurse, & one Matron in attendance, & only one wounded man, a Mexican citizen, accidentally shot in the left breast in hospital. The dispensary & storeroom are one & in good order—Wardroom only big enough for three beds—supplies ample. I condemned sundry stores and medicines as worthless and wornout. There is a small kitchen attached." It is not known if Captain Granger and Surgeon Smith took Mansfield's advice and moved the hospital to the vacant barracks.[101]

Since there was no artillery at Fort Lancaster, Mansfield found little need for an ordnance sergeant; however, Brenner was also serving as acting postmaster. Lieutenant Greene, a very busy man, performed all the duties of recruiting officer, commissary officer, and quartermaster. Both the Commissary and Quartermaster stores were well supplied. The baker was excellent, and the bread of the first quality. Lieutenant Greene was also responsible for the granary, hay yard, corral with twenty-three mules and three wagons, the carpenter's shop, and the blacksmith's shop. Lieutenant Greene's books and records were in order.

Mansfield was impressed with and complimentary of Captain Granger, reporting that he, "commands with ability, and satisfactorily, and is untiring in his efforts in the performance of his duties. He has repeatedly made efforts for a garden: and the past season by great labor, has succeeded in supplying his men with mellons, and Summer vegetables to a considerable extent. But all the plants had to be watered by hand. The discipline of the post is good."[102]

Impressed with what he found at Fort Lancaster, Mansfield recommended that the post be maintained. "It is a highly important position, in the midst of Indian depredations. About 6 weeks since two men were murdered by them about 10 miles off on the Pecos, and a few days since 4 Indians ran off 7 mules of the Stage Company, which has a station here. Numerous trains pass here & and very often they need assistance in repairs or supplies, which the Commanding Officer is obliged to for food and sometimes escorts. One Inft. Company however is ample here." However, Fort Lancaster would remain an active post for less than four months.[103]

As the year 1861 dawned, the nation was moving towards civil war. The prospect of a divided nation was particularly difficult for the regulars of the U.S. Army. Men from both the North and the South served together as friends. If Texas seceded, the federal posts would either have to be abandoned or defended, and the garrison of Fort Lancaster was vitally concerned about events over which they had no control. In February, news of the Texas Secession Convention and Act reached the frontier garrisons. On February 18, Bvt. Gen. David Twiggs, commanding the Department of Texas, surrendered federal property to the state. By the end of the month this news reached Fort Lancaster. General Twiggs, a native of Georgia and a Southern sympathizer, repeatedly requested instructions from Washington. When instructions were not forthcoming, Twiggs made his own decision, for which he was dismissed from the army on March 1, 1861.[104]

Special Order No. 32, dated February 24, called for the evacuation of the forts along the Lower Road. On February 27, Special Order No. 36 modified the previous command and instructed the garrisons of Forts Bliss, Quitman, Davis, Stockton, Lancaster, and Camp Hudson to "march upon the coast as soon as the means of transportation shall be received by them." Due to slow communications and the need for proper preparation, the officers and men at Fort Lancaster were not ready to leave until mid-March.[105]

On March 19, 1861, the officers and men of K Company, First Infantry, marched away from the fort they had established five and one-half years earlier. On that date Captain Granger filed his last *Post Return* from Fort Lancaster. The garrison consisted of the commanding officer, Lieutenant Greene, Lieutenant Haskell, Surgeon Smith, and seventy-three men. "The post was evacuated this day in compliance with Department Gen. Order No. 5 dated San Antonio, Texas, Febry 24, 1861 and Dept. S.O. No. 36 dated San

Antonio, Texas Feb. 27th 1861."[106]

Captain Granger filed one other *Post Return* under "Troops in Route, Comanche Creek, Texas." He reported that "Private Cunningham shot by David Ramsey an employee of the San Diego Mail Company on the 19th inst. a short time previous to the evacuation of the post."[107]

Fort Lancaster would never again be used as a garrisoned post of the United States Army. Initially the Confederates attempted to maintain the forts along the Lower Road, and each was assigned a small garrison. However, the logistics of supply and the need for manpower in the East were too much to manage. Eventually all the forts were abandoned, returning mastery of West Texas back to the Apache and Comanche.

In the fall of 1861, the Confederate Army of New Mexico passed along the Lower Road, camping at Fort Lancaster. The invasion of New Mexico, one of the more ambitious plans of the Confederacy, was lead by Brig. Gen. Henry H. Sibley. The plan was to conquer the Southwest and open the door to the wealth of California. After initial successes at the Battle of Valverde, and at Albuquerque and Santa Fe, Sibley was soundly defeated at the Battle of Glorieta Pass east of Santa Fe. The retreating column once again passed through Fort Lancaster on its return to San Antonio.

After the Civil War the Lower Road once again carried traffic, and in 1867 the army decided to re-establish some of the abandoned forts, but Lancaster was not among them. Occasionally travelers would camp on the grounds as the buildings fell into disrepair. Troops on patrol or using the road from San Antonio to El Paso would bivouac in the area. However, few would know, or remember, the vital service that had been provided by the handful of soldiers from the First Infantry Regiment—to patrol the road and to keep the communication link to California open during a crucial period in the nation's development.

NOTES

1. A. B. Bender, *The March of Empire: Frontier Defense in the Southwest, 1848–1860* (Lawrence: University of Kansas Press, 1952), 109.

2. Robert Utley, *Frontiersmen in Blue: The United States Army and the Indian, 1848–1865* (New York: Macmillan Co., 1967), 18; Bender, *The March of Empire*, 110–111; Fort Lancaster *Post Returns*, Jan.–Feb., 1856, Record Group 94, National Archives, Washington, D.C. (cited hereafter as NA).

3. J. D. B. Stillman, New York *Crayon* (Feb., 1856), 40–43.

4. Thomas T. Smith, "Fort Inge and the Texas Frontier Military Operations, 1849–1869," *Southwestern Historical Quarterly* (July, 1992), 3 (cited hereafter as *SHQ*); Robert Utley, *The Indian Frontier of the American West, 1846–1890* (Albuquerque: University of New Mexico Press, 1884), 39–46.

5. Utley, *Frontiersmen in Blue*, 18–21.

6. Edward Coffman, *The Old Army: A Portrait of the American Army in Peacetime, 1784–1898* (New York: Oxford University Press, 1986), 57, 68.

7. Bender, *The March of Empire*, 115.

8. Utley, *Frontiersmen in Blue*, 20–31.

9. Stillman, New York *Crayon* (Feb., 1856), 40–43.

10. Utley, *Frontiersmen in Blue*, 31–32.

11. Coffman, *The Old Army*, 92–96.

12. Utley, *Frontiersmen in Blue*, 22–23; Fort Lancaster *Post Returns*.

13. Utley, *Frontiersmen in Blue* , 42–45.

14. Ibid., 36; Bender, *The March of Empire*, 118; Utley, *Frontiersmen in Blue*, 40; Coffman, *The Old Army*, 138–141.

15. Inspector General Joseph Mansfield, *Inspection Report of Fort Lancaster*, Nov. 21, 1860, R.G. 94 (NA).

16. Randy Steffen, *The Horse Soldier*, Vol. II (Norman: University of Oklahoma Press, 1978), 5–65; Bender, *The March of Empire*, 116–117.

17. Inspector General Joseph Mansfield, *Inspection Report of Camp Lancaster*, June 9–11, 1856, R.G. 94 (NA); Utley, *Frontiersmen in Blue*, 25–27.

18. Thomas T. Smith, "U.S. Army Combat Operations in the Indian Wars of Texas, 1849–1861," *SHQ*, 99 (Apr., 1996), 503–507, 508–514.

19. Ibid., 530.

20. Mansfield, *Inspection Report*, 1860; Bender, *The March of Empire*, 121.

21. Fort Lancaster *Post Returns*; Bender, *The March of Empire*, 126–128; Utley, *Frontiersmen in Blue*, 38, 39 (quotation), 40–41.

22. Coffman, *The Old Army*, 107–108.

23. Ibid., 112–113; Mansfield, *Inspection Report*, 1856 and 1860.

24. Mansfield, *Inspection Report*, 1856 and 1860.

25. Mary M. Gordon, *Through Indian Country to California: John P. Sherburne's Diary of the Whipple Expedition, 1853–1855* (Stanford: Stanford University Press, 1988), 234–243; Stephen Thomas, *Fort Davis and the Texas Frontier: Paintings by Arthur T. Lee, Eighth U.S. Infantry* (College Station: Texas A&M University Press, 1976), 19; Coffman, *The Old Army*, 131–133.

26. Robert Utley, *Special Report on Fort Davis, Texas* (Santa Fe: National Park Service, 1960), 3.

27. William Goetzmann, *Army Exploration in the American West, 1803–1863* (New Haven: Yale University Press, 1965), 225–226; William Goetzmann, *Exploration and Empire: The Explorer and the Scientist in the Winning of the American West* (New York: Alfred Knopf Co., 1967), 273–274.

28. Goetzmann, *Army Exploration*, 227; Ralph Bieber, *Southern Trails to California in 1849* (Glendale, Calif.: Arthur H. Clark Co., 1937), 32–40.

29. Ralph Bieber and Averam Bender, *Exploring Southwestern Trails, 1846–1854* (Glendale, Calif.: Arthur H. Clark Co., 1938), 223–224.

30. Ibid., 260.

31. A. B. Bender, "Opening Routes Across West Texas," *SHQ*, 37 (Oct., 1953), 120; Kenneth Neighbours, "The Expedition of Robert S. Neighbors to El Paso in 1849," ibid., 58 (July, 1954), 37–54.

32. Ben Pingenot, "The Great Wagon Train Expedition of 1850," *SHQ*, 98 (Oct., 1994), 184; Goetzmann, *Army Exploration*, 231–232.

33. Francis Bryan, "Reports of Secretary of War with Reconnaissances of Routes from San Antonio to El Paso," Sen. Exec. Doc. No. 64, 31st Cong., 1st Sess. (1850), 21–26; Capt. George M. Wheeler, "Epitome of Warren's Memoir, 1800–1857, by Lieut. Gouverneur K. Warren," *Report Upon United States Geographical Surveys West of the One Hundredth Meridian, Vol. I* (Washington, D.C.: Government Printing Office, 1889), 567–571.

34. Bieber, *Southern Trails*, 32–40; Robert Schick, "Wagons to Chihuahua," *American West*, 3 (Summer, 1966), 72–79, 87–88.

35. Pingenot, "The Great Wagon Train Expedition," 183.

36. Ibid., 201.

37. John Russell Bartlett, *Personal Narrative of Explorations and Incidents in Texas, New Mexico, California, Sonora, and Chihuahua, 1850–1853* (Chicago: Rio Grande

Press, 1965), 113–114; and Goetzmann, *Army Exploration*, 198–200.

38. *Reports of Explorations and Surveys to Ascertain the Most Practical and Economical Route for a Railroad from the Mississippi River to the Pacific Ocean* (12 vols.; Washington, D.C.: A. O. P. Nicholson, Printer, 1854); Goetzmann, *Exploration and Empire*, 281–297.

39. Goetzmann, *Army Exploration*, 277–278, 291–292, 365–367.

40. Utley, *Special Report on Fort Davis*, 39–43.

41. Wayne Austerman, *Sharps Rifles and Spanish Mules: The San Antonio–El Paso Mail, 1851–1881* (College Station: Texas A&M University Press, 1985), 314–316; Emmie Mahon and Chester Kielman, "George H. Giddings and the San Antonio-San Diego Mail Line,"*SHQ*, 61 (Oct., 1957), 226–235, 318.

42. Roscoe and Margaret Conkling, *The Butterfield Overland Mail, 1857–1869*, Vol. II (Glendale, Calif.: Arthur H. Clark Co., 1947), 13; Ray Billington, *The Far Western Frontier, 1830–1860* (New York: Harper & Row, 1956), 279–281.

43. Robert Wooster, *Soldiers, Sutlers, and Settlers, Garrison Life on the Texas Frontier* (College Station: Texas A&M University Press, 1987), 50.

44. Utley, *Special Report on Fort Davis*, 19–22; Francis Heitman, *Historical Register and Dictionary of the United States Army* (Washington, D.C.: Government Printing Office, 1903), 613.

45. Dept. of Texas, Special Order No. 79, July 20, 1855 (quotation), R.G. 94 (NA); Fort Lancaster *Post Returns*, Aug., 1855.

46. Fort Lancaster *Post Returns*, Aug., 1855 (1st quotaton); Dept. of Texas, Special Order No. 79 (2nd quotation).

47. Heitman, *Historical Register*, 284, 825, 1040; William Powell, *List of Officers of the Army of the United States from 1779 to 1900* (New York: L. R. Hamersly and Co., 1900), 337.

48. Robert Wooster, *History of Fort Davis, Texas,* Professional Paper No. 34 (Santa Fe: Southwest Cultural Resources Center, 1990), 90.

49. *Texas Historic Forts, Architectural Research Reports, Part III, Fort Lancaster* (Austin: University of Texas School of Architecture, 1968), 22–23.

50. J. D. B. Stillman, New York *Crayon* (Feb., 1856), 40–43.

51. Ibid.

52. Ibid.

53. Ibid.

54 .Ibid.

55. Ibid.

56. Stillman, New York *Crayon* (Mar., 1856), 72–75.

57. Ibid.

58. Ibid.

59. Ibid.

60. Ibid.

61. Ibid.

62. Heitman, *Historical Register*, 469.

63. Mansfield, *Inspection Report*, 1856; M. L. Crimmins, "Colonel J. K. F. Mansfield's Inspection Report of Texas," *SHQ*, 42 (Jan., 1939), 122–148.

64. Mansfield, *Inspection Report*, 1856; Summary of Special Orders, General Orders, Letters Received and Letters Sent, The Department of Texas, 1855–1859, R.G. 94 (NA).

65. Mansfield, *Inspection Report*, 1856.

66. Ibid.

67. Ibid.

68. Ibid.

69. Lydia Spencer Lane, *I Married a Soldier; or, Old Days in the Old Army* (Albuquerque: Horn & Wallace, 1964), 44.

70. Department of Texas, Order No. 53, Aug. 21, 1856, R.G. 94 (NA).

71. Fort Lancaster *Post Returns*, Dec., 1856, Jan.–Feb., 1857; Heitman, *Historical Register*, 509.

72. Gordon, *Through Indian Country*, 11–15, 234–243.

73. John Sherburne, Letter to Chief Quartermaster of Texas, May 27, 1857, R.G. 94 (NA).

74. Ibid.

75. Ibid.

76. Ibid.

77. Ibid.

78. Lewis Lesley, *Uncle Sam's Camels: The Journal of May Humphries Stacey Supplemented by the Report of Edward Fitzgerald Beale, 1857–1858* (Harvard: Cambridge University Press, 1929), 156–157.

79. Ibid., 57 (quotation); Thomas, *Fort Davis and the Texas Frontier*, 19–21.

80. Lesley, *Uncle Sam's Camels*, 57.

81. Ibid.

82. Robert Wooster, *History of Fort Davis, Texas*, 95.

83. Robert Utley, *Special Report on Fort Davis*, 36–38; Wooster, *History of Fort Davis, Texas*, 96 (quotation).

84. Letters Received No. 342 (quotations), Dept. of Texas, 1855–1859, R.G. 94 (NA); Fort Lancaster *Post Returns*, Sept.–Nov., 1857.

85. Letters Sent No. 377 (quotations), Dept. of Texas, 1855–1857, R.G. 94 (NA); Fort Lancaster *Post Returns*, Sept.–Nov., 1857.

86. Dept. of Texas, Special Orders No. 138; Fort Lancaster *Post Returns*, Sept.–Oct., 1857.

87. Dept. of Texas, Special Orders No. 139, Oct. 27, 1857 (quotation); Dept. of Texas, General Order No. 33, Dec. 14, 1857, R.G. 94 (NA).

88. Dept. of Texas, General Order No. 33, Dec. 14, 1857.

89. Ibid.

90. Ibid.

91. Fort Lancaster *Post Returns*, Feb., 1858; Heitman, *Historical Register*, 582.

92. Fort Lancaster *Post Returns*, Apr.–Dec., 1858; Heitman, *Historical Register*, 475.

93. Fort Lancaster *Post Returns*, Mar., 1859.

94. Ibid., Apr., 1859.

95. Wooster, *History of Fort Davis, Texas*, 101–102.

96. Ibid., 102.

97. Fort Lancaster *Post Returns*, July–Dec., 1859.

98. Inspector General Joseph Mansfield, *Inspection Report of Fort Lancaster*, Nov. 21, 1860, R.G. 94 (NA).

99. Ibid.

100. Ibid.

101. Ibid.

102. Ibid.

103. Ibid.

104. Utley, *Special Report on Fort Davis*, 45.

105. Dept. of Texas Special Order No. 36, Feb. 27, 1861, *War of the Rebellion: A Compilation of the Official Records of the Union and Confederate Armies*, Ser. I (Washington, D.C.: Government Printing Office, 1880), I, 596.

106. Fort Lancaster *Post Returns*, Mar., 1861.

107. Ibid.

BIBLIOGRAPHY

Austerman, Wayne R. *Sharps Rifles and Spanish Mules: The San Antonio–El Paso Mail, 1851–1881.* College Station: Texas A&M University Press, 1985.

Bartlett, John Russell. *Personal Narrative of Exploration and Incidents in Texas, New Mexico, California, Sonora, and Chihuahua, 1850–1853.* Chicago: Rio Grande Press, 1965.

Bender, A. B. "Opening Routes Across West Texas." *Southwestern Historical Quarterly,* 37 (Oct., 1933).

———— *The March of Empire: Frontier Defense in the Southwest, 1848–1860.* Lawrence: University of Kansas Press, 1952.

Bieber, Ralph. *Southern Trails to California in 1849.* Glendale, Calif.: Arthur H. Clark Co., 1947.

Bieber, Ralph and A. B. Bender. *Exploring Southwestern Trails, 1846–1854.* Glendale, Calif.: Arthur H. Clark Co., 1938.

Billington, Ray. *The Far Western Frontier, 1830–1860.* New York: Harper & Row, 1956.

Bryan, Francis T. "Reports of the Secretary of War with Reconnaissances of Routes from San Antonio to El Paso." Sen. Exec. Doc. No. 64, 31st Congress, 1st Session.

Conkling, Roscoe and Margaret. *The Butterfield Overland Mail, 1857–1869.* Glendale, Calif.: Arthur H. Clark Co., 1947.

Department of Texas. Military Records including General Orders, Special Orders, Correspondence Received and Correspondence Sent, 1855–1861. Washington, D.C.: Record Group 94, National Archives.

Fort Lancaster *Monthly Post Returns.* Washington, D.C.: Record Group 94,

National Archives.

Goetzmann, William. *Army Exploration in the American West, 1803–1863.* New Haven: Yale University Press, 1965.

——— *Exploration and Empire: The Explorer and Scientist in the Winning of the American West.* New York: Alfred Knopf Co., 1967.

Gordon, Mary M. *Through Indian Country to California: John P. Sherburne's Diary of the Whipple Expedition, 1853–1854.* Stanford: Stanford University Press, 1988.

Heitman, Francis. *Historical Register and Dictionary of the United States Army.* Washington, D.C.: Government Printing Office, 1903.

Lane, Lydia Spencer. *I Married a Soldier; or, Old Days in the Old Army.* Albuquerque: Horn & Wallace, 1964.

Lesley, Lewis B. *Uncle Sam's Camels: The Journal of May Humphreys Stacey, Supplemented by the Report of Edward Fitzgerald Beale, 1857–1858.* Cambridge: Harvard University Press, 1929.

Mahon, Emmie and Chester Kielman. "George H. Giddings and the San Antonio-San Diego Mail Line." *Southwestern Historical Quarterly,* 61 (Oct., 1957).

Mansfield, Inspector General Joseph K. F. *Inspection Report of Fort Lancaster,* June 10–11, 1856. Washington, D.C.: Record Group 94, National Archives.

——— *Inspection Report of Fort Lancaster,* November 21, 1860. Washington, D.C.: Record Group 94, National Archives.

Neighbours, Kenneth. "The Expedition of Robert S. Neighbors to El Paso in 1849." *Southwestern Historical Quarterly,* 58 (July, 1945).

Ormsby, Waterman. *The Butterfield Overland Mail.* Edited by L. H. Wright and J. M. Bynum. San Marino: Huntington Library, 1942.

Pingenot, Ben E. "The Great Wagon Train Expedition of 1850." *Southwestern Historical Quarterly,* 98 (Oct., 1994).

Pope, John. "Report of a Route for the Pacific Railroad, Near the Thirty-second Parallel, Lying Between the Red River to the Rio Grande." *The Pacific Railway Surveys,* Vol. II. House Exec. Doc. No. 91. Washington, D.C.: A. O. P. Nicholson Printing, 1855.

Powell, William. *List of Officers of the Army of the United States from 1779 to 1900.* New York: L. R. Hamersly and Co., 1900.

Schick, Robert. "Wagons to Chihuahua." *American West,* 3 (Summer, 1966).

Sherburne, John P. "Letter to the Chief Quartermaster of Texas, Major D. H. Vinton, Fort Lancaster, May 27, 1857." Washington, D.C.: Record Group 94, National Archives.

Smith, Thomas T. "Fort Inge and Texas Frontier Military Operations." *Southwestern Historical Quarterly*, 96 (July, 1992).

———— "U.S. Army Combat Operations in the Indian Wars of Texas, 1849–1881." *Southwestern Historical Quarterly*, 99 (Apr., 1996).

Steffen, Randy. *The Horse Soldier, 1776–1943*. Vol. II. Norman: University of Oklahoma Press, 1978.

Stillman, J. D. B. Letters Published by the New York *Crayon*. February and March, 1856.

Thian, Raphael P. *Notes Illustrating the Military Geography of the United States, 1813–1880*. Edited by John M. Carroll. Austin: University of Texas Press, 1979.

Thomas, Stephen. *Fort Davis and the Texas Frontier: Paintings by Arthur T. Lee, Eighth U.S. Infantry*. College Station: Texas A&M University Press, 1976.

Texas Historic Forts Architectural Research Reports, Part III, Fort Lancaster. (Submitted to Texas Parks and Wildlife Dept.) Austin: University of Texas School of Architecture, 1967.

Utley, Robert. *Frontiersmen in Blue: The United States Army and the Indian, 1848–1865*. New York: Macmillian Co., 1967.

———— *Special Report on Fort Davis*. Santa Fe: National Park Service Southwest Regional Office, 1960.

———— *The Indian Frontier of the American West, 1846–1890*. Albuquerque: University of New Mexico Press, 1984.

War of the Rebellion: A Compilation of the Official Records of the Union and Confederate Armies. Series I, Vol. I., Washington, D.C.: Government Printing Office, 1880.

Wheeler, Captain George M. "Epitome of Warren's Memoir, 1800–1857," by Lt. Gouverneur K. Warren. *Report upon United States Geographical Surveys West of the One Hundredth Meridian*. Vol. I. Washington, D.C.: Government Printing Office, 1889.

Wooster, Robert. *History of Fort Davis, Texas*. Professional Paper No. 34. Santa Fe: Southwest Cultural Resources Center, 1990.

———— *Soldiers, Sutlers, and Settlers: Garrison Life on the Texas Frontier*. College Station: Texas A&M University Press, 1987.

About the Author

Lawrence John Francell is a museum services consultant who lives in Fort Davis. He is a volunteer at Fort Davis National Historic Site and is an adjunct lecturer in the Museum Studies Department of Baylor University.